Contents

TECHNIQUES OF ROUTING

Techniques of Routing

Jim Phillips

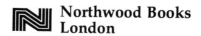 Northwood Books
London

Published 1980

© Northwood Publications Ltd and Jim Phillips, 1980

86
ISBN 7198 2680 0

A 'Building Trades Journal' book

Printed and bound in Great Britain by
The Garden City Press Ltd, Letchworth, Herts.

1. Basic principles of the router

The router is now considered to be one of the most versatile machines used in the wood, plastics, and light-metal working trades. Few know who introduced the first router, since it evolved gradually from a rotary drill or cutter operated by hand. History illustrates man's resourcefulness in improving output, from a bow drilling device used as early as 10,000 B.C. (see Fig. 1.1) through to the achievement of the modern-day hand router. This book is designed to give the many tradesmen who own a hand router or intend to buy one, the benefit of practical experience and useful tips from trade users and craftsmen.

Fig.1.1. Even in 10,000 B.C., Stone Age man was striving and finding ways of using his hands more effectively.

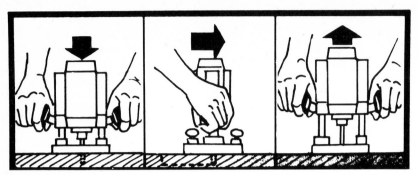

Fig.1.2. Basic principles of the plunging router, (Left to right) Plunge in and lock. Rout the groove. Release lock and spring up.

Many applications and suggestions may be 'old hat' to some tradesmen, but experience in the field has shown quite definitely that many firms have a thirst for knowledge about the capabilities of the hand router. Few firms offer satisfactory instruction manuals, even though the routing machine, if used to full advantage, will both increase production and drastically reduce labour costs.

The arrival of the 'plunging' type router in the 1940s caused a ripple of interest in the woodworking trade, but the then high cost of such routers with spring-loaded bases, prevented them from being generally accepted in the trade. Today, however, such routers as the Elu, with its ease of operation, and competitive price (close to that of a conventional hand router), are fast becoming standard equipment in the woodworking trades. Furthermore, with the price barrier removed, the more professional type of amateur is taking up routing as a constructive leisure occupation.

While we are praising the merits of the latest 'plunge' type routers, it should be stated here and now, that in no way are we depreciating the skill and fine work of craftsmen who have used the conventional router for over four decades. In skilled hands, these routers produce work equal to their modern counterparts.

There are numerous benefits in using a 'plunging' router, but the fundamental advantages are as follows:

Safety aspects

Factory inspectors are encouraging the use of routers with this plunging action, and the safety aspects almost speak for themselves. When the 'plunging' router is used portably, the cutter only projects below the base when the operator is actually engaged in routing, i.e. when the router carriage is depressed, and the cutter is in the work. After each operation the carriage lock is released and the cutter retracts out of harm's way.

Simplicity

From experience, it has been found that semi-skilled labour with a modicum of commonsense, can use a 'plunging' router. The basic principle is shown in Fig. 1.2. With a few minutes teach-in, and a half hour or so practice, the elementary concept of setting up to do a job is mastered. The sequence of preparing the machine for work and actually operating it, becomes second nature very quickly.

Improved finish

The advantage of being able to position the base of the router firmly on the work-piece and to plunge the cutter down at 90 deg. is the all-important factor. It means a clean, square cut entry into the work and, similarly, when the routing job is completed, the retraction of the cutter at 90 deg. prevents any inclination to chip out the top surface. It is this confidence in being able to cut squarely that enables an operator to perform so quickly and yet accurately.

Good vision for working

The open type carriage of the 'plunging' router provides more room for changing the cutters, introduction of spanners, etc. Furthermore, when the 'plunging' router is depressed, the vision for sighting the work is excellent. It is important for the operator to see what he is doing at all times, when to start and when to stop.

Applications

To describe the advantages and workings of the more progressive
plunging router, we shall portray one such router generally accepted
and used in the trade by woodworkers and craftsmen alike; this is the
Elu MOF 96. It has a speed of 24,000 rpm, and is rated at 3/4 hp. It has a
plunging depth of up to 2in. and weighs approximately 6lbs. There are
a number of larger models in the range, which work on the same
principle. The ones we shall be mentioning from time to time are the
MOF 31 and 98, which have 1,200 and 1,600 Watt motors respectively.
Heavy-duty applications in the woodworking trades require more
powerful routers to perform the work satisfactorily, and these models
can take wider and deeper cuts in one pass of the router.

Setting up the router ready for work

For the purpose of this section, we shall describe a well proven light
duty hand router, the Elu MOF 96 (see Fig. 1.3). Heavy duty models
working on similar principles will be mentioned in later chapters.

The first step in setting up the router is to fix the cutter (see Fig. 1.4),
but before fitting (or extracting) them always remove the electric plug
from socket point. After ensuring that collet nut (9) is loose, the
appropriate cutter is inserted into the collet (9A). Tightening the cutter
involves holding motor spindle (9B) with 13mm open ended spanner
and tightening the collet nut gently (no force) with 17mm spanner
(both supplied with standard equipment). The standard collet
supplied with this machine has a ¼in. (6.35mm) diameter opening to
accept cutters with ¼in. diameter shanks. A wide range of cutters are
available, and these are illustrated and described in the Appendix.

To set the required depth of cut, without switching on the motor,
depress the router on its spring loaded columns, until the tip of the
cutter rests on the workpiece: then lock the router in that position by
turning the plunging knob (6) a quarter turn clockwise.

Now adjust the depth of cut by sliding the depth bar (5) to the
required position, and lock thumb screw (7). The distance between the
base of the depth bar (5) and the screw head on the rotary turret stop (8)
will be the depth to which the router will cut. Allow motor to spring
back to original position by turning knob anti-clockwise. Router is now
ready to cut at the pre-set depth. Three alternative depths may be
pre-set using the rotary turret stop, see page 85.

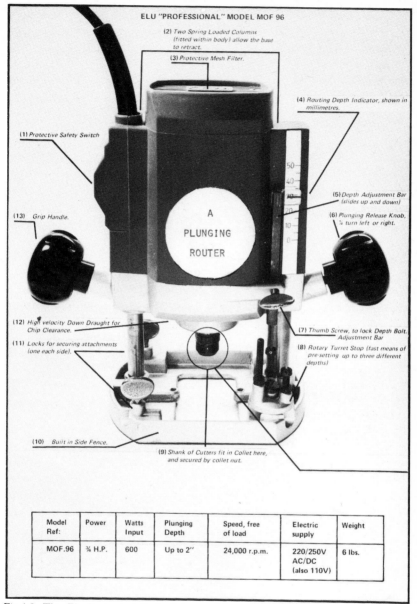

ELU "PROFESSIONAL" MODEL MOF 96

(2) Two Spring Loaded Columns (fitted within body) allow the base to retract.

(3) Protective Mesh Filter.

(4) Routing Depth Indicator, shown in millimetres.

(1) Protective Safety Switch

(5) Depth Adjustment Bar (slides up and down)

(13) Grip Handle.

(6) Plunging Release Knob, ¼ turn left or right.

(12) High velocity Down Draught for Chip Clearance.

(11) Locks for securing attachments (one each side).

(7) Thumb Screw, to lock Depth Bolt. Adjustment Bar

(8) Rotary Turret Stop (fast means of pre-setting up to three different depths)

(10) Built in Side Fence.

(9) Shank of Cutters fit in Collet here, and secured by collet nut.

Model Ref:	Power	Watts Input	Plunging Depth	Speed, free of load	Electric supply	Weight
MOF.96	¾ H.P.	600	Up to 2″	24,000 r.p.m.	220/250V AC/DC (also 110V)	6 lbs.

Fig.1.3. This Elu Router is typical of the new 'plunger' type routers, its main features are described above.

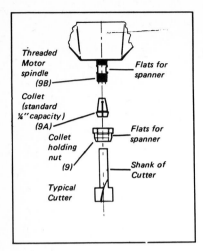

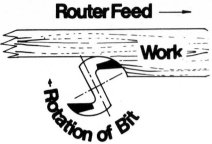

Fig.1.4. (Left) The cutter fixing system is clearly illustrated in the exploded view.

Fig.1.5. (Above) The router should be fed in the opposite direction to that which the cutter is rotating.

To commence work

First switch on the motor (at switch (1)) and depress the router once more until the cutter has reached its full stroke, which has been pre-set by the depth stop. Without releasing hold on the handles, a quarter clockwise turn of the knob (6) will secure the motor in the depressed position. Routing can now commence, but note well, the router should be fed in the opposing direction to that in which the cutter is rotating (see Fig. 1.5).

When the routing operation is completed, the same knob (6) is given a quarter turn anti-clockwise, which allows the router head to spring up squarely from the workpiece. Work is now completed, and the motor should be switched off.

2. Main applications

Grooving

There is a misconception that router accessories are costly, indeed the most important device, namely the adjustable side fence, is normally part of the standard equipment, as with the Elu. Grooving, rebating, moulding and recessing can all be carried out using this one accessory. Grooving is one of the most popular applications for a hand router. No other method can produce a clean-cut and accurate slot so quickly. When making shelves, a routed groove ensures a good fit, especially if made slightly undersize.

For grooving narrow boards, a side fence (see Fig. 2.1) should be fitted to the machine to run against the long edge of the workpiece. For

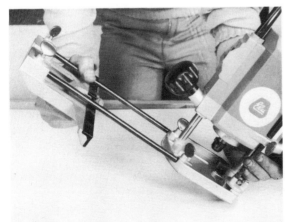

Fig.2.1. The adjustable side fence slides into the router base.

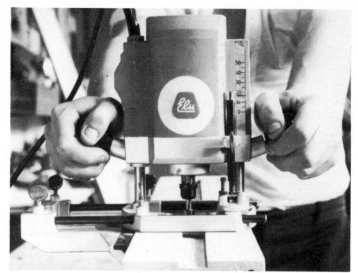

Fig.2.2. (Above) A drawer side needs a groove for the runner. The side fence, part of standard equipment, is used to advantage.

Fig.2.3. (Below) The router, with side fence fitted, was used to run a small groove along the edge of this casement window, for the insertion of weather stripping. Cutter Ref 3/4, 8mm ϕHSS was used.

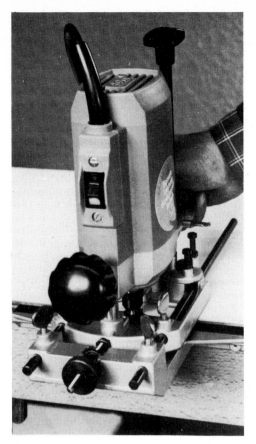

Fig.2.4. The lateral fine adjuster offers a more delicate means of feeding in the side fence. It locates between the two rods on the fence and slots into a groove on the router base.

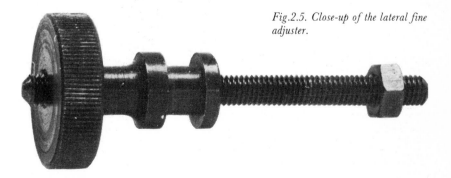

Fig.2.5. Close-up of the lateral fine adjuster.

Fig.2.6. The router is fitted with an extension, made from thin plastic. This ensures that the router continues on its parallel path, when leaving the workpiece. Note the 'overcut' board to support the side fence, which assists the process, and prevents chipping out when cutting across the grain.

example, a drawer side needs a groove for the runner (see Fig. 2.2) and a casement window needs a small groove for the insertion of weather stripping (Fig. 2.3). A useful accessory for adjusting the groove width, is a fine adjuster screw feed (see Figs. 2.4 and 2.5).

When using a side fence care should be taken to avoid cutting out of true when finishing the run to the end of the board. A safety measure which can be taken to guard against this is to fit an extension to the inside of the side fence (using the two pairs of screws securing the plastic liners). This can be made of thin plastic or plywood (see Fig. 2.6). An 'over-cut' board is also necessary. This serves two purposes; it allows the side fence to continue along its parallel path, and at the same time prevents the cutter chipping out as it leaves the workpiece and enters the 'over-cut' board; this is most important when machining across the grain.

When grooving on large flat surfaces, for example, a paired set of bookshelf sides (see Fig. 2.7), the whole process is assisted if a home-made grooving board (see Fig. 2.8) is used, since the housings can be lined up squarely and clamped. It can be used, not only for

Fig.2.7. A shelf unit, strong and of pleasing appearance, is a perfect way to show the value of the router in furniture construction.

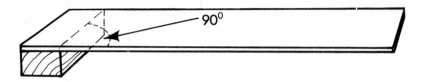

Fig.2.8. A grooving board greatly facilitates marking out and clamping.

Fig.2.9. A pair of stop groove housings being routed out from a single sheet.

Fig.2.11. (Below) Corners cut back.

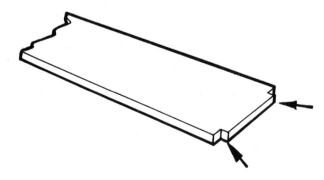

marking the positions of the housings out squarely, but also as a runner or guide, along which the router will pass when grooving (see Fig. 2.9). If the routed groove stops before the board edge is reached, not only is a pleasing finish obtained, but also the shelf can be cut back approximately ¾ in. to allow for any shrinking in the shelf width (see Figs. 2.10 and 2.11).

Fig.2.10. An exact matching pair of housings for a shelf unit. Note the routed grooves have stopped before the board edge is reached.

Fig.2.12. Rebating a window to accept a second glazing panel, is shown being done with the Elu router.

Rebating

Rebating for double glazing has great potential in the building and maintenance trades, particularly where house conversions and modernisations are concerned. If window frames are to be rebated after manufacture, or existing windows double glazed the procedure is as follows: first remove them and place them flat downwards on the workbench. An angular block is made (see Fig. 2.12) and fitted to the side fence in such a way that the cutter is proud of the corner, but no more than the depth of the rebate required. The router is guided round the internal edge of the frame, and by adjusting the depth of cut, the right amount of material can be removed to enable the second pane of glass, or complete double glazed unit, to be inserted. A wide cutter (ref. 4/2, Appendix page 130) to take the full rebate is recommended, with several passes to reach the required depth.

Fig.2.13. (Above) Here is an accurate and fast way of cross halving and tee halving joints with a router. The battens are side stacked and clamped.

Fig.2.14. (Below) Battening will all be identically cut, if clamping has been carefully carried out previously, and router passed squarely across the material.

Machining half-lap joints (see Figs. 2.13 and 2.14) is an excellent example of a time-saving application for the router. Battens are grooved and rebated at predetermined positions for the production of the framework. The battens are lined up accurately and clamped together on one edge, then the 'plunge depth' of the router is set to half that of the batten. Using a clamped on straight edge, the router is then passed across the battens to the required depth and width.

Ideally, a cutter whose width is equal to the batten width should be chosen, so as to limit the number of passes. However, the number of passes needed depends also on the power factor of the router. When using $1\frac{1}{2}$in. by $\frac{3}{4}$in. battening, for example, a 3/4 hp router would need six passes, a $1\frac{1}{2}$ hp router four passes, and a 2 hp router two passes. Naturally, this is for approximate guidance only, but emphasis should be on making a clean cut without overloading the motor. The tone of the motor will indicate whether or not you are doing this.

Fig.2.15. Multi-mould effects obtained by varying the depth of cut; full use being made of the wide variety of mould cutters now available (see Appendix).

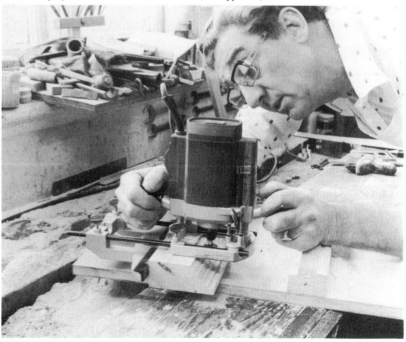

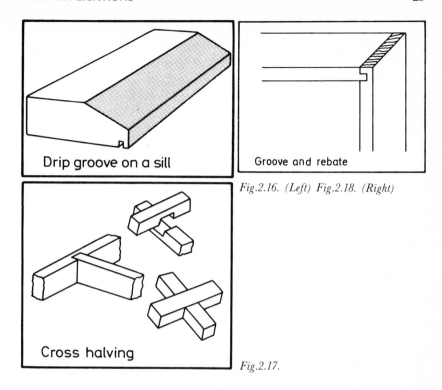

Drip groove on a sill

Groove and rebate

Fig.2.16. (Left) Fig.2.18. (Right)

Cross halving

Fig.2.17.

Other machining operations

It is not generally realised that multi-mould effects can be achieved by taking a number of passes at different depths and widths, resulting in a very attractive finish. The temptation to take too much material off in one pass must be resisted. The mould shown in Fig. 2.15, was obtained by taking up to six passes, with the outer edge being machined before the inner part. Maximum advantage was taken of the rotary depth stop to reach a new depth in seconds; this most attractive feature of the 'plunge' router is discussed on page 10.

By selecting the right cutter shape and size, a number of additional grooving and rebating operations may be undertaken. To name a few:

   (a) Drip grooves under edge of window sill or door (see Fig. 2.16);
   (b) Grooved joints for batten framework (see Fig. 2.17);
   (c) Combination groove/rebate to obtain a good joint (see Fig. 2.18);

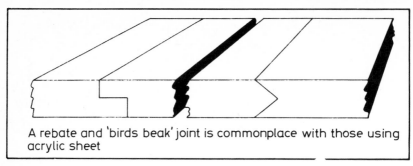

A rebate and 'birds beak' joint is commonplace with those using acrylic sheet

Fig.2.19.

(d) Rebate and 'bird's beak' joints for joining acrylic sheet (see Fig. 2.19);

(e) Drop-leaf table made using two separate cutters (see Fig. 2.20).

Fig.2.20. A drop-leaf table is created by using concave and convex cutters to ensure an exact fit. Cutters are shown in the Appendix, pages 123 and 124.

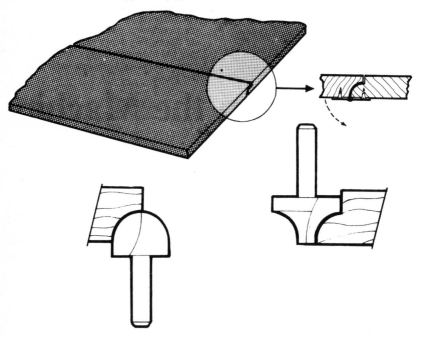

Panelling

While moulded sections can be 'planted' on flat surfaces, 'panelling' here refers to work where the router is applied direct to the board face. Man-made boards do not lend themselves to this application unless the workpiece is to be painted, but natural timber, especially hardwood, can be most attractively panelled out with the careful use of cutters now available. (Cutters suitable for this purpose are illustrated in the Appendix on pages 129, 130, 131 and 137.)

Fig.2.21. A typical example of panelling work using an ovolo cutter. The plunging router with its 90 deg. entry is invaluable for the central mould work.

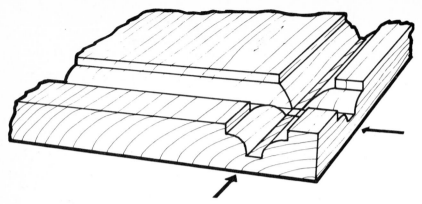

Fig.2.22. This clearly shows the attractive effects of straight parallel cuts using radiused cutters in conjunction with a straight edge.

For internal moulds (see Fig. 2.21), when no lead-in from the sides is possible, the 'plunge' router is invaluable. It ensures a 90 deg. entry and a continuity in the moulded edges without imperfections. The same cutter is used to profile an ovolo mould, with only the side of the cutter engaging on the board edge. The router used in Fig. 2.21 was a heavy duty model Elu MOF 98, rated at 1,600 Watts; with this model, the panelling cut was grooved out in one pass. This is preferable to making several passes with a smaller, lower rated machine. It does not mean, however, that a 3/4 hp router, for example, could not be used for this purpose, but extra care would be required. The temptation is to take too heavy a 'bite', which would overload the motor and reduce the number of revolutions, resulting inevitably in a poor finish.

Parallel cuts can be made with the side fence of the router if the moulded panel cuts are reasonably close to the edge, otherwise straight edges or a template sheet can be used. When the mould runs off the edge on the cross grain (see Fig. 2.22) an over-cut board is essential to avoid the grain splitting out. Always use a fence extension as well, to maintain the router on an even path.

A multi-panelled door provides an excellent opportunity to produce attractive and unusual effects. The influx of cheap imported doors from the Far East should be a stimulus for original thinking for designs in moulded panelling work. The latest range of mould cutters shown in

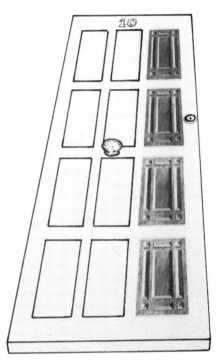

Fig.2.23. Example of attractive panelling on a front door. Straight routing cuts are used with radiused grooving cutters of various dimensions. A straight edged batten is used instead of the side fence.

the Appendix offers such possibilities. One idea for a front door is to introduce small panel inserts, each insert having a criss-cross panel shape to provide a unique effect (see Figs. 2.23 and 2.24).

3. Freehand work

Freehand patterns and shapes can be cut expertly in the surface of thick material with surprisingly little practice. Freehand work can best be described as using the router without a guide fence, guide bush or other aids. The design is first marked out on the surface, preferably with a felt pen. The router is placed in position, the motor is switched on and the cutter is plunged into the workpiece to a pre-determined depth (use the adjustable depth bar). This technique of freehand cutting in practised hands, is clearly shown by the cut-outs made on

Fig.3.1. A typical application of deep freehand work by a firm of insulation contractors. A heavier duty router, namely the model Elu MOF 31, was used to plunge through the 2 in. thick material. A hand jigsaw would have 'run out' at the bottom edge, due to the thickness.

Cutters in the 3 group and 4 group range can be supplied with 50mm length of cut. These cutters, used with the Elu router which has deep plunging facilities, provide the right combination to solve the problem.

Fig.3.2. The router being used as a 'jigsaw'. With a little practice, one can become quite an expert in following a marked form. With a light duty router, however, one should limit the thickness of the board to 6mm, so as to avoid cutter breakage.

soft insulation board to recess steel R S J's, and pipework (see Fig. 3.1). If thin material is involved, one can cut right through and use the router as a 'Jigsaw' (see Fig. 3.2).

Examples of freehand grooving work

A typical freehand grooving operation, which is often done with a router, is the cutting of house names into plaques (see Fig. 3.3). More often than not, such work in commercial circles is done with a

Fig.3.3. Routing 'house names' in a rough sawn oak panel.

Fig.3.4. (Below) An illustration of freehand work. The hand router is being used to create a 'how to get there' message. Freehand engraving in solid hardwood can be a most absorbing pastime, and in skilled hands, most effective.

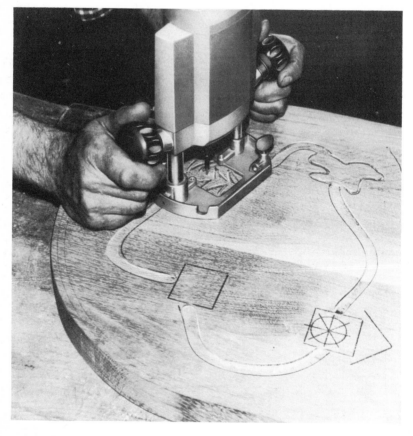

template, when a guide bush is fitted. Template routing is a subject which deserves full attention, and Chapter 4 is devoted to it.

Another illustration of freehand work (Fig. 3.4) shows the hand router being used to create a 'how to get there' message. Freehand engraving in solid hardwood can be a most absorbing pastime, and in skilled hands, most effective.

The fine depth adjuster

Sometimes, for such work as engraving, fine adjustment is needed. For this purpose, a fine depth adjuster (see Figs. 3.5 and 3.6) is fitted in place of the depth adjustment bar (Fig.1.3.(5)). This fixes to studding on the turret depth stop (Fig.1.3.(8)).

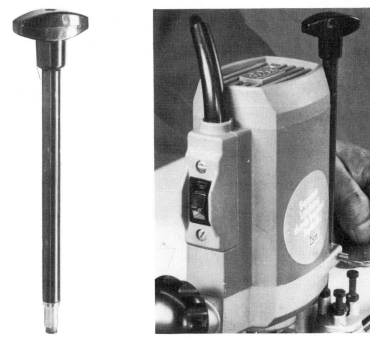

Fig.3.5. (Left) The fine adjuster above can be fitted in place of depth adjustment bar. This provides a slow feed for such work as engraving.

Fig.3.6. (Right) The fine depth adjuster (Fig.3.5.) is rotated clockwise and anti-clockwise to bring the cutter up and down approximately 1 mm per full turn.

Edging work

Freehand bevelling, moulding and rebating can be carried out, even on shaped edges, by using cutters with guide pins mounted on their bases (see Fig. 3.7). The procedure for using these cutters is to set the depth so that when the guide pin is resting on the edge of the board, the cutter engages on the top corner edge of the board. To sum up, the guide pin of the cutter acts as the guide, and, if care is used, a well formed bevel or mould can be produced on the edge in a remarkably short space of time. Practice runs on scrap wood are recommended, so as to learn the technique. If too much pressure is exerted the guide pin will score or burn the edge of the workpiece. In the sign-making trade, these cutters are used extensively for bevelling acrylic, and operators have developed great expertise. See also pages 124-6.

Often it is found to be more convenient to manipulate the workpiece against the cutter. For this purpose, the router is inverted with the cutter protruding through the table top (Fig. 3.8). A special profiling table can be bought for this purpose, although a home-made one can be fabricated. Routing tables, or light 'spindles' as they are known in the trade, provide for a number of useful machining possibilities. These will be described in Chapter 9.

Fig.3.7. (Left) Freehand edge moulding using a radius cutter with guide pin follower.

Fig.3.8. (Right) The router has been inverted and fitted to a table stand. With a chamfer cutter projecting through the table, a signmaker is seen putting a bevel on a letter 'E' made from acrylic.

Fig.3.9. The beam trammel slides into the slots on the router base and is shortened or lengthened to adjust the radius.

Fig.3.10. (Below) Circular patterns cut into wood and acrylic show the unlimited possibilities open to those with artistic trends.

Circular work

The trammel bar, or scribing arm as it is sometimes called, see Fig. 3.9, offers numerous possibilities for decorative flat and inlay work. Shaped articles can be cut out, and attractive mould features produced (see Fig. 3.10). A fine example of this is shown in Figs. 3.11 and 3.12, where a grandfather clock face is under construction. Most attractive geometric shapes (see Figs. 3.13-3.17) and curves can be made with a little imagination.

When engraving work only is involved, the depth stop is adjusted to give a shallow cut, but if extra fine adjustment is needed, the depth bar is replaced by a fine adjusting rod (see Fig. 3.5). If rotated clockwise or anti-clockwise, it lowers the cutter slowly in and out of the work. (It locates into the turret depth-stop head.) If deep grooving is involved, the procedure is to set the turret stop to cut in stages. Each completed circle would require the turret stop to be rotated to allow the router to cut to a greater depth. Carried one stage further, this system can be used to cut right through the material (see Fig. 3.18). Articles such as round table tops and wooden tableware can be cut without using a template (see Fig. 3.19). Edges can be moulded by merely substituting the grooving cutter with a moulding cutter, but the same centre point must be retained.

Fig.3.11. (Above) The beam trammel or scribing arm is used with the Elu MOF 96 to cut a series of arcs at different depths. The workpiece is to be the upper part of a grandfather clock (See Fig.3.12.).

Fig.3.12. (Below) The clock face in a more advanced stage of construction.

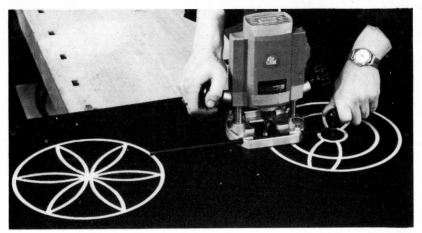

Fig.3.13. Attractive geometrical shapes for an inlay can be engraved when a beam trammel is used for the radius work.

Fig.3.14. A more complicated geometrical design.

Fig.3.15. A decorative wall panel being made from high density blockboard. One flute, radius and ovolo cutters were used. See Appendix.

Figs.3.16.3.17. Further examples of attractive engraving work using the beam trammel of the router.

Fig. 3.18. (Above) By adjusting the depth of the router in stages, the beam trammel can be used to cut out a table top, bread board, or just an attractive wall plaque.

Fig.3.19. (Left) Table tops can be cut, moulded and trimmed if the same fulcrum point is used throughout.

Fig.3.20. A protective sheet of plywood is fitted to table top with double sided tape. This protects the table top being marked with the fulcrum point of the beam trammel.

A useful tip to avoid marking the surface of the workpiece with the centre point of the trammel bar, is to fix a thin piece of plywood on to the work surface (see Fig. 3.20). It can be secured with double-sided adhesive tape. In this way the fulcrum point of the bar is pressed into the plywood rather than the work surface. When the work has been completed, the plywood is removed.

Router/lathe workshop

A most productive and creative device is now available to extend the use of hand routers. It is generally described as a router/lathe onto which light duty routers (maximum 6lbs) can be clamped in place. In Fig. 3.21 the Elu MOF 96 router is shown clamped onto a router/lathe. The depth adjustment knob is an important feature, since fine adjust-

Fig.3.21. The Elu MOF 96 router is seen fitted to the 'Woodmaster'. Note the depth adjustment knob for fine adjustment of height, a most important feature for lathe cutting work, as a steady feed-in is necessary to obtain a good finish. The 600 watt motor of the Elu router allows for a relatively heavy cut to be made in one pass.

ment of height and steady feed-in is necessary to obtain a good finish. The separate components of the router/lathe can be seen in Fig. 3.22. The workpiece, which commences as a square section of wood, is fitted between tailstock and headstock. The hand router is fitted by bolts to the carriage. Adjustable stops limit the lateral stroke to suit applications, the carriage sliding on the two uppermost rails. The hand crank turns the workpiece, and if the index pin is engaged, the carriage slides

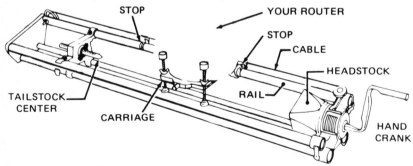

Fig.3.22. The router/lathe is illustrated with the main features described. The workpiece, which commences as a square section of wood, is fitted between tailstock and the headstock. The hand router is fitted by bolts to the carriage. Adjustable stops limit the lateral stroke to suit applications, the carriage sliding on the two uppermost rails. The hand crank turns the workpiece and, if the index pin is engaged, the carriage slides simultaneously along the guide rails.

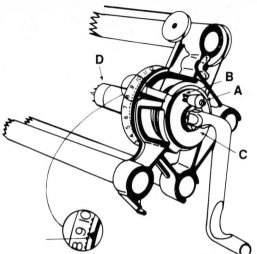

Fig.3.23. A = indexing pin.
B = slot to receive index pin.
C = drum housing which
houses cable. D = spiked
engaging head (this is re-
moved and driven into work-
piece centre point).

Fig.3.24. A number of attractive shaped legs. The lines adjacent to some of the drawings show the shape required if a template pattern is used.

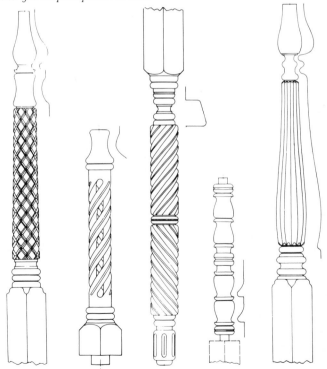

simultaneously along the guide rails. The indexing head is illustrated fully in Fig. 3.23 to show the scale setting.

Three basic operations can be performed: turning; lateral fluting and beading; and a combination of fluting, cutting and turning.

In turning operations the workpiece is rotated by the cranked handle. The routing machine is manually slid along the carriage (with an optional template for working to a pre-shaped pattern).

Lateral grooving may be carried out in 24 different positions, utilising the indexing head which is located within the headstock.

By using a combination of the above two operations spiral and 'roping' patterns can be obtained. In this instance the indexing head is used together with the auto-cable drive. Cranking the handle turns the workpiece and drives the carriage along the slides simultaneously. These spiral and roping cuts are done in multiples of 12, 8, 6 or 4 equidistant passes through 360 deg. In this way most attractive chair or table legs can be produced (see Fig. 3.24).

4. Templates and jigs

Without doubt, it is the use of templates which offers the widest scope of applications for the router. There is literally no limit to the possibilities available, and it is this point which creates a challenge to the craftsman. Commercially it offers the woodworker a fast and efficient means of increasing his output. Template jigs are a more sophisticated means of guiding the router to perform various functions and we will discuss these on page 49.

Templates are usually made from hardboard, plywood or plastics, the harder the better. Thickness should be between 6mm and 10mm since if they are too thin, there is the possibility of the guide bush slipping out of the template while working, thus spoiling the work. Much ingenuity can be used in the construction of templates, varying the shape and size in accordance with the workpiece. They can be clamped down in a number of ways, by G clamps or toggle clamps or, better still, stuck down with tape. The use of double-sided tape is most effective for this purpose, since the work itself is not marked, and the working area is left completely clear of encumbrances (see Figs. 4.1 and 4.2).

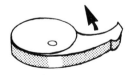

Fig.4.1. Eccentric swivel clamp.

Fig.4.2. Toggle clamp.

There are certain rules to be adopted with the guide bush system, whether an inside or outside template is used. Templates must be cut to size, bearing in mind the space between the guide bush and the cutting edge.

How to assess the size of the template

For the purpose of this exercise, we have chosen a typical application, namely sinking of a flush handle (see Fig. 4.3). The procedure is as follows:

1. Choose a cutter of small diameter to match as near as possible the radius of the corner of the handle (this will reduce the need to clean up the corners with a hand chisel afterwards

2. Choose a guide bush with clearance inside for the cutter to rotate without rubbing. See Fig. 4.4, showing projection of cutter through guide bush.

3. Subtract the diameter of the cutter from the outside diameter of the

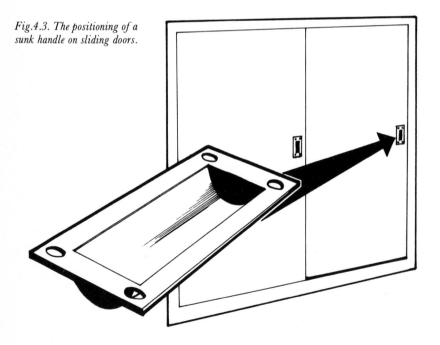

Fig.4.3. The positioning of a sunk handle on sliding doors.

Fig.4.4. Router, showing guide bush fitted to base. Standard bush supplied is 24mm dia., but other sizes are available — 17mm., 27mm. and 30mm. dia.

Fig.4.5. The sketch shows the system for working out the size of the template, relative to the guide bush diameter and cutter diameter.

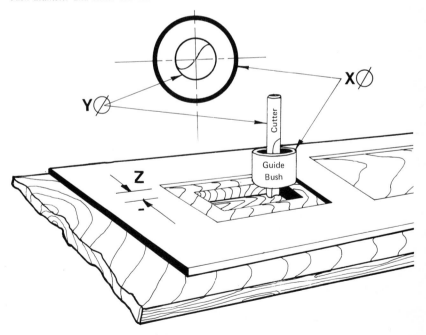

bush and divide by two. This will indicate how much larger the template should be in relation to the size of the part being recessed. Refer to Fig. 4.5 for clarification.

X.   This is the outside diameter of the bush.
Y.   This is the diameter of the cutter.
Z.   This denotes the extra amount to be allowed when cutting out the template.

Special note: The *left* aperture in the template shown in Fig. 4.5 is for recessing the centre deep part of the handle. The right aperture in the template is to recess the outer shallow handle plate.

Types of templates

A variety of template systems will be discussed, some suitable for short runs of work, others intended for batch production in a factory, where speed and maximum output are the priorities. By adopting these professional methods the amateur can extend the use of his router to a surprising degree.

How to apply the router

After the cutter and selected guide bush have been fitted, the router is

Fig.4.6. (Left) The router base and guide bush, showing the cutter projecting through it.

Fig.4.7. (Right) A template jig for slotting out mortises.

placed on the template surface with the guide bush side pressed against the template edge. The motor is then switched on and the router depressed and locked there. The cutter is now protruding through the centre of the bush to the pre-set depth (see Fig. 4.6). Now follow the contour of the template, maintaining the pressure of the guide bush against the template edge throughout until work is complete.

A template for mortising

Apart from dovetail joints and dowel joints, mortises and tenons can be effectively cut with the plunge router. A simple template is made as described on page 43, and is fitted over the workpiece (Fig. 4.7). A two flute cutter to match the size of the mortise is a natural choice. It is advisable to take several 'bites' to clear swarf and prevent overload. The problem of the rounded corners in the mortise is best solved by rounding the corners of the tenon, but those who prefer a square tenon, can cut the mortise corners square with a chisel. Tenons can be made most efficiently on the router table; see Chapter 10.

Fig.4.8. This template was used to make the back splats of a Chippendale reproduction chair. The left side was routed out first, then it was reversed to obtain a replica for the right side.

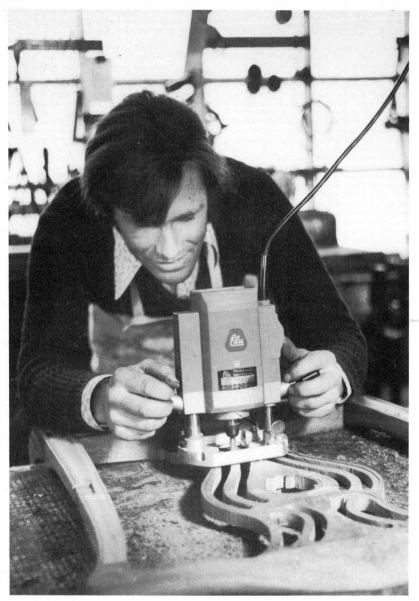

Fig.4.9. Surfacing the back of a Chippendale reproduction chair, using back and forward movements with the cutter depth set for shallow rout. A hand router series was used extensively to produce the shaped back and top of this chair.

Reproduction work

Craftsmen reproducing period furniture cannot afford to ignore the unique cutting facilities of the router. Those who revere the craftsmen of bygone days are inclined to scorn this particular power tool, but the many hours of hard chiselling work which it saves would have relieved even Chippendale! Fig. 4.9 shows free-hand surfacing of the chair back of a Chippendale reproduction.

The use of templates for the curvature work is most interesting. The template for the back splats, shown in Fig.4.8. was applied in two stages. It was first used to shape the left part, and then reversed to shape the opposite side identically. We should mention that the operator seen using the router in Fig. 4.9 is Nigel Batchelor, who was awarded first prize in woodcraft, at the Woodworker Exhibition in London. The chairs, which he produces for his own company, take approximately four weeks to construct. Much of the hardwood used for such reproduction work is reclaimed timber from old buildings and furniture.

'Sinking' hardware fittings

Cleverly designed factory-made templates can be purchased for production work. These are primarily designed to sink hardware fittings, such as locks, fasteners, and pivots, used in the more sophisticated continental type windows. The one in Fig. 4.10 has interchangeable panels which clip into place in a matter of seconds. The template frame is available in various forms; it can be clamped onto the surface or onto a door edge for sinking hinges and lock plates.

The interchangeable panels are supplied blank for firms to cut out the shapes they need for recessing their ironmongery. Some progressive ironmongery manufacturers, produce hardware fittings (e.g. hinges) with rounded corners, so no 'cleaning up' of corners with a chisel is needed.

Staircase template jig

The Trend clamp-on jig illustrated in Fig. 4.11, greatly facilitates the

Fig.4.10. This factory-made template jig has interchangeable panels with slots to suit iron-mongery fittings, such as barrel locks, lock plates and window fasteners.

routing out of housings to receive the treads and risers of staircases. These routing jigs are produced principally for use with all industrial hand routers and are extremely accurate. Only the first tread and riser need be marked out which presents a considerable saving in time.

The template basically is constructed from 10mm dense plastic which is extremely rigid and completely resistant to distortion. It is 24in. × 20in., and is supplied complete with a fully adjustable and reversible fence, together with a screw feed clamp. A sub-base, which can be fitted to all hand routers, is fitted with an adjustable slider plate or follower; this locates in the template slots when routing. The jig design automatically allows for wedges of a normal thickness to be introduced.

One means of selecting the right cutter for use with a staircase jig, is to measure the timber to be used for the tread and deduct $\frac{3}{8}$in. (9.5mm). This denotes the diameter of the cutter to be chosen. Another handy guide for cutter selection, is shown below (references are to cutters in the Appendix, page 127).

For tread thickness	Suggested cutter ref.
$\frac{7}{8}$in.	32/1
1in.	32/2
1$\frac{1}{8}$in.	32/3

Homemade template for staircase work

A template cut from plywood can be constructed to speed up the cutting out of treads and risers (see Fig. 4.12). However, great care

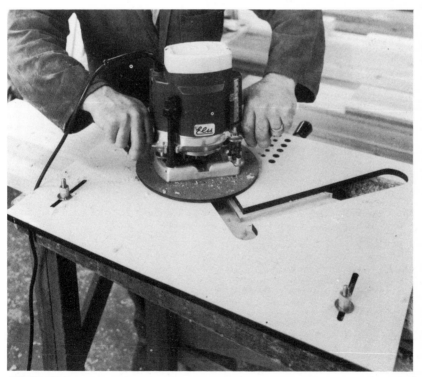

Fig.4.11. A heavy duty router, MOF 31, is seen cutting stair housings through a special template jig.

Fig.4.12. Stair housings are routed out with this home-made template device, which is clamped to the workpiece.

should be taken in pre-marking out the paths the router will take, as minor discrepancies on the template will multiply by the time the staircase is completed. The factory-made template described previously precludes the need for marking out in advance of cutting (except for the first housing).

Fig.4.13. A heavy duty plunge router is seen cutting letter box openings. An alloy template is used for the pattern.

Templates for building applications

The cutting out of letter box openings in a 20mm thick plywood panel presents an excellent application for the router. True, it could be done with a drill and jigsaw, but the joy of the router in such an application, is the repetition of a clean cut and accurate finish, with minimal cleaning up required after the job is completed.

Fig. 4.13 shows a series of letter box openings being cut through a 'master' template, made from duralium. A heavier duty router was used to make the cut out in one pass, but the MOF 96, a smaller version, could have been used for this purpose, making three passes in order to plunge through. Once again the advantages of the plunging action and rotary depth stops come into their own.

Louvred windows and doors

Templates are often used for repetitive grooves, or housings as they are generally termed; making housings for louvres is a typical application. A conventional and craftsmanlike method of setting up to produce louvred housings, is to produce a plywood template, as seen in Fig. 4.14 which provides a series of stopped grooves. The template is secured by panel pins or double sided tape. As each set of housings are produced through the template, it is moved to a new position.

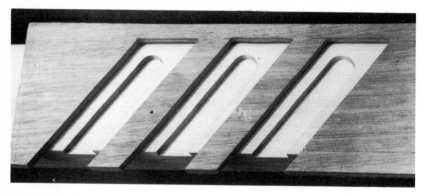

Fig.4.14. A template designed for routing out housings, in the construction of louvred door panels.

Louvre template jig

It is when repetition work is involved that template jigs become an essential aid for production. For high output, the essence of the problem is to produce as many identical housings as possible in a given time. One method of achieving higher production is to use a sliding box template, on the lines sketched in Fig. 4.15.

Artistic shapes

With the Elu router portrayed here, a number of sizes of guide bushes are available (see Fig. 4.4). These, in conjunction with inside cutting

Fig.4.15. For making louvred doors, a sliding 'box' template provides a useful means for routing out the end housings at predetermined spacings.

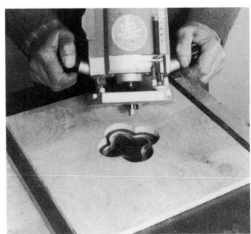

Fig.4.16. Attractive shapes being routed through an 'inside' template.

or outside cutting templates, offer numerous possibilities, particularly of an artistic nature. Attractive panels and cut-outs can be produced when making chairs, desks, and cupboards, etc. Two examples are shown in Figs. 4.16 and 4.17.

Panelling work on say, cupboard doors, is a typical use for simple rectangular templates (see Fig. 4.18). Using some of the latest Ovolo, Ogee and Classic shaped cutters (see Appendix, page 130), unusual and attractive effects can be obtained. By alternating the guide bushes and cutters, intricate mould shapes can be produced.

Fig.4.17. Pattern being copied by using 'outside' template.

Fig.4.18. Using a simple rectangular template, preferably made from hard plastic material, panelling can be produced with attractive results. By using different radiused cutters, a variety of effects can be achieved.

Extrusion jig for cutting and drilling aluminium

One of the thriving and growing facets of the building trade has been the introduction of aluminium extrusions for door and window construction. It has been the use of plunging type routing techniques which have made the fabrication work so economical. Without such innovations, the construction with extrusions would be extremely labour intensive.

The machine shown in Fig. 4.19 is the clamp-on routing jig, and is just one of a number of such machines which vary in sophistication and output. This machine, namely the Elu Ref SAL 54, is ideally for batch production runs in window and door construction. Whilst home made templates can be made for these applications, generally speaking the standard of work produced from them is inferior. Machining of aluminium and other non-ferrous metals requires complete rigidity of both template and workpiece. The principle on which these clamp on machines work is as follows:

A metal template to match the slots required is fitted within the framework. In operation the routing jig is fitted over the aluminium window or door and clamped, using the special eccentric clamp provided and gauging the position with the side or length stops. The router is then switched on and depressed so that the cutter penetrates the workpiece. When the router is locked in position it is guided along the sliding framework (laterally and transversely) until the cut is completed. The knob is then given a quarter turn anti-clockwise, to enable the router head to spring out of the work.

This routing device is extremely efficient and fast in operation. It is powered by a single-phase, 600 Watt motor, with a free running speed of 20,000 rpm. A more automated machine which produces a higher output is also now available.

A number of cutters are available for machining aluminium (these are illustrated in the Appendix, pages 135, 142, ref. groups 47/2, 47/20, 50). Most of them have single spiral geometry, and are capable of drilling, slotting and profiling aluminium extrusions in one operation (page 135). These cutters, made from special high speed steel, are ideal for recessing keyholes and hardware fittings when used at speeds between 10,000 and 24,000 rpm.

It is recommended that a lubricant stick is applied to the workpiece, or a mist spray to the cut, during operation. In this way, a clean burr free cut can be achieved. Certainly, attention to such details will extend the life of the cutters.

Cutting aluminium transoms

Using the router in the way illustrated, trimming the ends of extrusions for producing transoms and mullions can be undertaken most efficiently. It should be mentioned that this is an inexpensive way of producing machined end sections, there being more sophisticated machinery to cut transoms on a production basis. The hand equipment, described here, consists of a hand powered router, supplied as a set which includes hard wood runners, into which the extrusions slide, a cross runner bar, toggle clamps to hold the material, and a special tungsten carbide tipped router cutter, which is designed to rebate the

Fig.4.19. Slotting holes and keyways in aluminium frames is just one more job for the Plunge Router. The machine shown is an Elu model SAL 54. It is only a 2 minute operation to slot and drill the extrusion ready to receive the lockset.

Fig.4.20. Transom cutter in action, cutting the end of an extrusion.

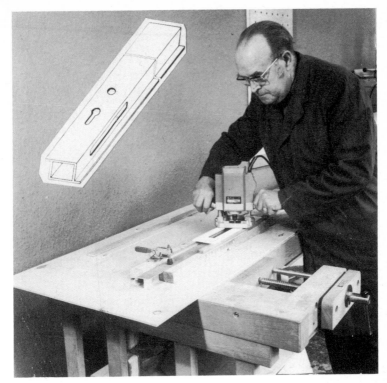

Fig.4.21. A home-made template set up for clamping and slotting the extrusions.

extrusion ends, leaving a clean cut finish (see Fig. 4.20). (The cutter is illustrated in the Appendix, page 142.) The action is fast, and no cleaning up is required.

Slotting and drilling aluminium

While there is a special purpose-made jig for cutting slots in extrusions (see page 59), a home-made template with clamps and guides, similar in some respects to the transom set-up, can be used to drill and slot, e.g. for making keyholes and recesses to accept lock plates (see Fig. 4.21). The sections should be held rigid if vibration and the consequential poor finish is to be avoided.

5.   Use with plastics

Those who have tried trimming Formica edges by hand will know how difficult it is to obtain a professional finish. In this chapter we shall describe how the Elu router can carry out such work at considerable speed and leave a clean cut edge with no cleaning up being required whatsoever.

Trimming the edge (vertical) lips first

For straight edges, it is the normal practice to use narrow strips of plastic to form the edge lippings. These should be glued in place, preferably allowing no more than 3mm of the edge to project above the board edge.

It is important that the edge strip should be glued and trimmed *before* the top sheet is fitted. This will ensure that the top plastic surface is not marked or spoilt by the under edge of the cutter when trimming the lips flush with the board top.

Setting up the router for edge lipping

The fine vertical adjuster is fitted to the router (in lieu of the depth rod), and engaged by the threaded screw on the rotary depth stop. A suitable cutter for trimming the lipping is shown in the Appendix, page 142. It has a bottom cut as well as a side cut, enabling it to be used for trimming the overlay, which is discussed overleaf.

The adjuster disengages the plunge spring action, and if it is rotated clockwise, the cutter will plunge deeper. Depth is set just to skim along the (uncovered) top surface, with the centre of the cutter aligned over the vertical lipping (see Fig. 5.1). Before actually commencing to trim the lipping, make a test run on a piece of scrap wood, with an off-cut of plastic fitted to it (secured by double-sided tape). With practice this procedure becomes unnecessary, but at first a little experience is essential.

Preparing for trimming the overlay top

Assuming the vertical lipping has been trimmed flush with the top surface, the overlay on the plastic top is now ready for fitting. The procedure is as follows:

The laminate sheet is cut and glued in place with approximately $\frac{1}{8}$in. overhang. Excess glue should be removed, as this could become a hindrance when cutting. Once the glue has hardened, the edge can be trimmed back. Assuming a 90 deg. cut edge is required, a square edged

Fig.5.1. Trimming the vertical lipping, using the side fence and depth adjuster to gauge the correct amount to remove.

Tungsten tipped cutter is fitted to the router. This should be cutter ref. 47/2 (shown on page 142), the bottom edge of which was used to trim the lipping.

While the vertical adjuster is still left in position and used to bring the cutting edge down to the required position, the fine adjuster on the side fence is all important for trimming the top surface correctly. This will provide the means of obtaining that close trimmed edge, so important for a really professional finish.

Trimming the overlay

The machine is positioned over the work and the cutter brought down until the face of the cutting edge lines up with the laminate surface. The side adjuster gives the final position but until experience has been obtained in setting up, it is a good plan to make some trial runs to ensure that the machine is set correctly. Trim from left to right as shown in Fig. 5.2.

Fig.5.2. Trimming the plastic overlay, using the side fence and fine lateral adjuster to bring the cutter in parallel with the underlying edge.

Fig.5.3. Trimming the overlay and slotting the board edge simultaneously is now possible. A special trimming set is available for this purpose. The Elu MOF 31 is seen performing this operation on a 'kidney' shaped coffee table.

Combined trimming and slotting

A slot can be made in the edge of a table top or sideboard at the same time as the overlay is trimmed (see Fig. 5.3). Assuming the plastic top has not been trimmed, cutter ref. 47/1 (page 141 in Appendix) has the facility to trim the edge at 90 deg., and slot the edge simultaneously to accept a 'keyed' or barbed edge strip. The slotter is bolted to its base in much the same way as the slotter is fitted to the 33/9 arbor. It is necessary to make some trial runs to ensure the slot is central. Edge strips should be tight fitting and gently tapped into position with a mallet after glueing (see Fig. 5.4). It is advisable to choose an undersize slotter (one size below tongue thickness).

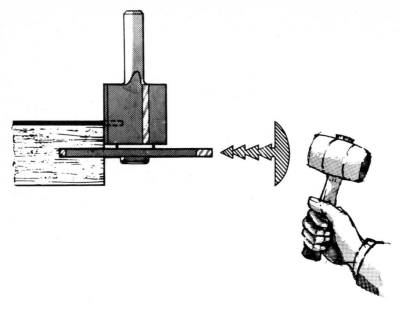

Fig.5.4. Trimmer 47/1 and Slotter 47/7. This trimming cutter has a combination facility. It will trim and slot a recess for a 'barbed' edge strip, which is then tapped into the slot.

Trimming shaped panels

Trimming the lips of shaped panels can present a problem, but a special trimming cutter is available for this purpose (see Fig.5.6). Fig. 5.5 shows a table top being trimmed with a trimmer ref. 46/2 (page 138 in Appendix). This cutter has a bearing mounted on its base, the same diameter as the cutter. By dispensing with the side fence, the roller on the cutter follows the shape of the panel and the cutter above it trims the laminate cleanly and accurately. Note, however, that the board edges should be smooth, since any imperfections will be reflected in the laminate edge.

Panels faced on both sides

When boards are faced on both sides with laminate, the edges can be speedily flushed with a trimmer which is designed to cut both edges simultaneously. The cutter is made in two parts, with a bearing guide in the centre (ref. 46/7, page 138).

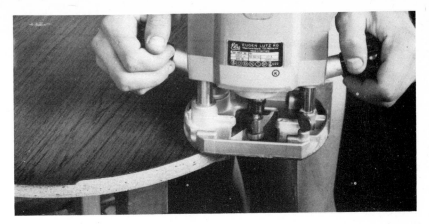

Fig.5.5. Trimming the plastic overlay on this table top, presents no problem if a trimmer with guide roller type 46/2 is used. The surface edge of board should be smooth, as imperfections could be reflected in the plastic edge.

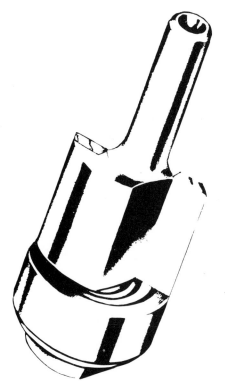

Fig.5.6. (Left) This trimmer with helical flutes and tungsten tipped, trims the laminate overlay, with the bearing on its base guiding its path. (Right) This double trim cutter removes top and bottom edges simultaneously. The central bearing engages on the board edge.

Fig.5.7. A plunge and trim TC cutter is being used to cut out 'pockets' of laminate. The cutter has a follower on its base to ensure that the cutter follows the correct path.

Cutting out 'pockets' in the overlay

Inset sinks and basins obviously need apertures to accept soap dishes, wastes, taps or overflows. The normal procedure is to first cut out the apertures in the underlying board, glue the plastic overlay down and then cut out the 'pockets' under the laminate covering. The means of doing this, with the plunge router, is to 'pierce' drill the laminate over the pocket, and cut out the aperture using cutter type ref. 47/4 (page 140 in the Appendix). Fig. 5.7 shows the action of this cutter which cuts the laminate, using the smooth end part of the cutter to follow the shape of the underlying board.

Flushing hardwood lipping

One simple means of trimming hardwood edge strips is to set up the router so that the base of the cutter trims the hardwood strip flush to the top surface. In Fig. 5.8, one can see the Elu MOF 31 router trimming

Fig.5.8. (Above) Trimming the hardwood lipping, flush with the top surface, is done with a router fitted with an adjustable edging attachment.

Fig.5.9. (Left) This fine lateral 'screw feed' offers fine adjustment when exact position for trimming is required. The 'guide' roller follows the board edge — ideal for trimming shaped table tops, etc.

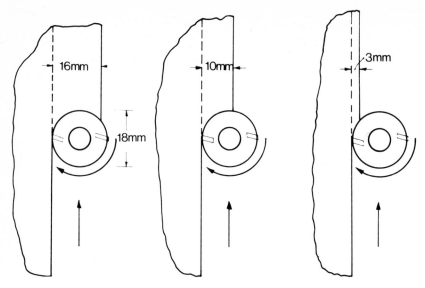

Fig.5.10. If you limit the projection of the plastic edge, so a minimum of material is removed, this will drastically extend the life of the cutter. Left to right, incorrect — better — correct.

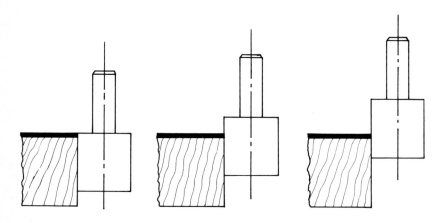

Fig.5.11. Useful tip to extend the life of cutters: a longer life for the cutting edges can be obtained if the trimming depth is varied. Introducing bevel trimmers at different heights will also spread the wear of the cutting edges.

edge strips. It is provided with a fine adjuster (see Fig. 5.9), enabling the cutter to be set in exactly the position required (overshooting would spoil the surface). With these fine adjustments on the vertical and horizontal plane, edge strips can be cut accurately and cleanly with a minimum of cleaning up after the work is completed.

Tips for extending cutter life

The projection of the overhang of laminate should be minimal, as overhang in excess of 3mm can cause cutter wear to increase by as much as 400 per cent. The sketches in Fig.5.10 show how to avoid unnecessary cutter wear.

Another tip which gives longer life from the cutters is to adjust the depth of the cutter regularly when trimming the laminate top surface. In this way it is possible to spread the wear on the cutter most effectively. Fig.5.11 shows this recommendation clearly.

6. Joints and tenons

Dovetail joint

A dovetail joint is usually recommended as the most secure one. To test this claim a colleague and I performed an interesting experiment. Using a small dovetail cutter (ref. 31/2, page 127 in Appendix), a six-inch-long dovetail groove was cut in a Sapele hardwood block (see Fig. 6.1). Then a dovetail tongue to match the groove was made in a section of chipboard, using the same cutter (see Fig. 6.2). The fine adjuster on the side fence was used to obtain the exact width needed.

The dovetail tongue was then slid into the dovetail groove using hand pressure only. The block was then attached to a ceiling joist and my colleague, 10 stone in weight, lifted himself off the ground. The joint was examined afterwards, and no stress or fatigue break-away,

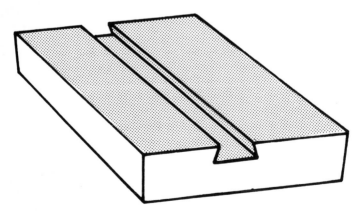

Fig.6.1. The dovetail groove, so immensely strong, as proven by the experiment described on this page.

Fig.6.2. A dovetail tongue being cut in the chipboard panel; the subject of the experiment described on page 72.

was apparent. Clearly a dovetail joint, even without glue, nails or screw fixings, provides a most secure means of jointing one piece of material to another. An added advantage is that framework, shelving and the like, can be disassembled; a useful asset when moving house.

Dovetail template jigs

Nowadays commercially produced furniture rarely has joints made on the dovetailing principle, due mainly to the high cost of machining work. However, the desire for hand made furniture with a craftsman-like quality and appearance is steadily increasing.

Fig.6.3. (Above) Dovetailed corner joints under construction, using the Elu MOF 96 router and the dovetail template jig.

Fig.6.4. (Below) The dovetail tightness is adjustable by raising the cutter up or down with the fine adjuster on the router. A depth gauge is supplied with each dovetail machine, and the illustration shows a gauge being used to obtain correct cutter projection.

Furniture manufacturers have sophisticated automatic dovetailing machines, but the amateur and small joiner can make use of the dovetailing jigs currently available. If these are used to produce sets of drawers, they are likely to last a lifetime, bearing in mind the remarkable strength of dovetail joints. Full instructions on how to use such jigs are supplied by the manufacturers, but the basic principles are described below.

The dovetail jig illustrated in Fig. 6.3 shows an Elu MOF 96 router, cutting dovetail joints, 8mm deep, in parana pine, which are to be used for drawer sides. After clamping the material in position, the guide bush on the router base runs within the dovetail fingers, with the cutter protruding in its centre (see Fig. 6.4). If the cutter is set at the correct depth using the gauge provided, the two dovetail members can simply be tapped into position prior to glueing (see Fig. 6.5).

Fig.6.5. The router has cut an identically matching set of dovetail tongues and grooves for jointing this drawer front and side together.

Tongueing and grooving

The making of tongued and grooved flooring is a simple operation when a router is combined with an arbor (see Fig. 6). (Arbors are discussed fully in Chapter 9). A set of grooves with TCT cutting edges has now been designed specifically for use with all overhead routing machines and heavy duty hand routers, used portably or inverted as a 'mini-spindle'. These groovers are suitable for running at speeds of between 7,000 and 20,000 rpm. The tongue/groover set incorporates two four-winged TCT groovers and an arbor with adjustable spacers (see Fig. 6.7). The sets are available with arbors, having ¾in. or ½in. diameter shanks. The tongue is produced by using the 6mm and 10mm groover in tandem. The groove to receive the tongue is made with the 6mm groover.

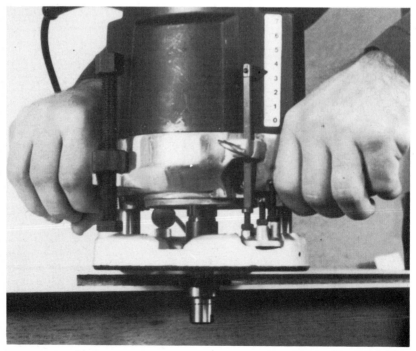

Fig.6.6. The application shown above for the arbor and groover is a 'natural' for making tongued and grooved flooring.

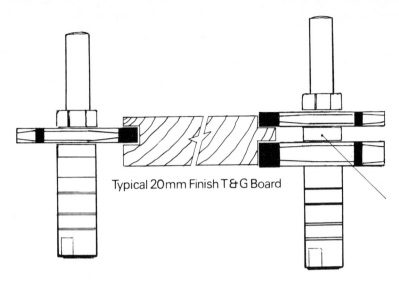

Typical 20mm Finish T & G Board

Fig.6.7. Cutters for tongueing and grooving: ref. 334.

Fig.6.8. Routing machine table with a sliding mitre fence.

Fig.6.9. The batten is rebated to form a tenon. The end of the cutter machines both sides squarely and cleanly.

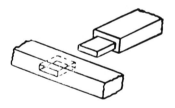

Fig.6.10. Diagram to show how the tenon fits into its socket.

Fig.6.11. The finished tenon — clean and squarely cut.

Making tenons

With the router inverted and fitted beneath the table, small tenons can be cut cleanly and quickly using the sliding facility of the mitre fence (see Figs. 6.8 and 6.9). This fence is set at 90 deg. to the direction of cut. A sliding board is introduced to facilitate the forward movement when making the tenon. In operation, the batten to be tenoned is laid across the board with the end butting up against the adjustable side fence. It is held firmly against the mitre fence with the left hand.

The cutter used for this operation must have a 'bottom-cut' and is set to protrude vertically to the thickness of the tenon. It will be noted from Figs. 6.8 and 6.9 that the main fence is fitted with a flat strip; this is to allow the stub of the tenon to slide without hindrance. To cut the tenon, the mitre fence, sliding board and batten, are passed in the direction of the arrows, so that the batten end is trimmed by the cutter. The batten is then turned over to cut the opposite side and complete the tenon (Fig. 6.1).

Dowel drilling

Dowel jointing (see Figs. 6.12 and 6.13) is a useful means of jointing and can be carried out by the plunge drilling router. A simple jig is made for sinking dowel holes. Standard dowels are used for the tenons (dowel $\emptyset$ = cutter $\emptyset$). The template jig used has equally spaced drilled

Fig.6.12. By making a simple drilling jig with holes to match the bush size on the router base, drilling holes for dowel joints is both fast and effective.

Fig.6.13. An angular type clamp-on jig can be fitted over mitred corners to 'plunge' a series of apertures which will accept 8mm Ø dowels.

holes, 17mm Ø. These match the projecting guide bush diameter (17mm Ø O D) on the router base. If care has been taken to make the plywood jig, repetition jointing on a commercial scale is feasible. An angular type clamp on jig can be fitted over mitred corners to 'plunge' a series of apertures to accept 8mm Ø dowels.

7. Heavy duty applications

In this chapter we shall be portraying the heavier duty model in the Elu range, namely the MOF 98, 1,600 Watt plunge router, which will be of particular interest to those concerned with the heavy duty applications which are often encountered in the building trades.

Construction of heavy duty router

Figs. 7.1 and 7.2 show the basic construction of the router, which is fairly similar to its smaller counterpart, namely the Elu MOF 96. The main variations are the locking mechanism and the introduction of an adjustable height lock, which is completely independent of the depth lock bar (6). The depth locking lever is pressed to plunge the router down, and released to lock it in that position. Figs. 7.1 and 7.2 are self explanatory, most points having been discussed in the commentary on the smaller model in the range (which can be found on page 11).

Setting to a given depth

Figs 7.3-7.5 describe the basic points for setting the router to reach to a given depth.

In this sequence, the routing depth A is portrayed as being sufficiently shallow to groove the work in one plunge. For example, a 16mm groove could be cut easily at 12 or 14mm depth, bearing in mind the power of the 1,600 Watt motor. However, when routing to greater depth, the rotary turret stop becomes invaluable.

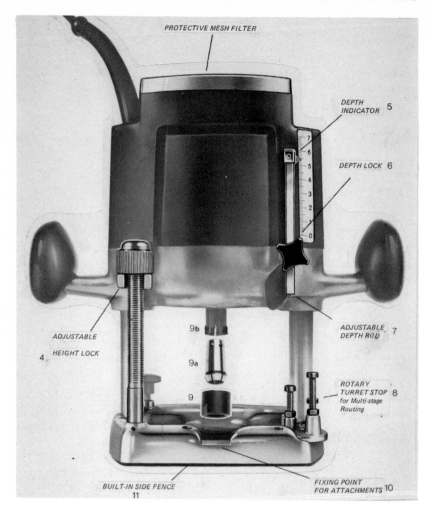

Fig.7.1. The main features of 'plunge' router MOF 31. The depth setting system is clearly illustrated.

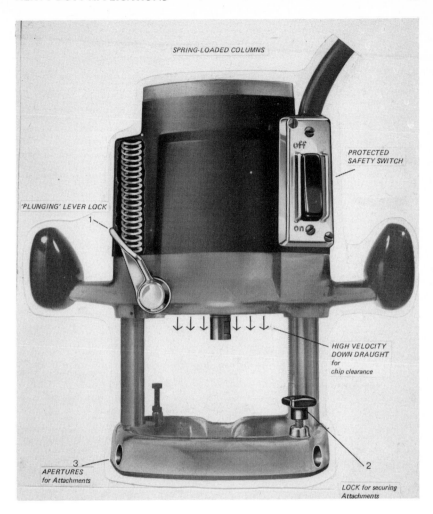

SPRING-LOADED COLUMNS

PROTECTED
SAFETY SWITCH

'PLUNGING' LEVER LOCK

1

HIGH VELOCITY
DOWN DRAUGHT
for
chip clearance

3
APERTURES
for Attachments

2

LOCK for securing
Attachments

Fig.7.2. This plunge router has spring-loaded columns. Release of plunge lever locks the router in the depressed position.

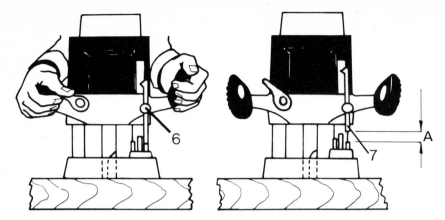

Fig.7.3. (Left) Loosen depth lock (6) and see that the depth rod (7) is free. Then depress plunge lever and carriage, so that the cutter rests on the workpiece. Now release lever so that router is locked down in that position.

Fig.7.4. (Right) Set the depth rod (7) so that the space between its base and the turret stop equals the depth of cut needed for the operation (A). Then tighten depth lock (6), depress lever to allow carriage to spring up.

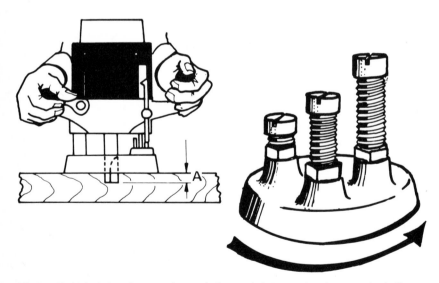

Fig.7.5. (Left) Switch on the motor, depress the lever and plunge router to the pre-set depth. Carry out the routing operation.

Fig.7.6. (Right) The set screws on the depth stop are in three lengths, but are themselves adjustable in height to provide the exact depth stop position to suit the operation.

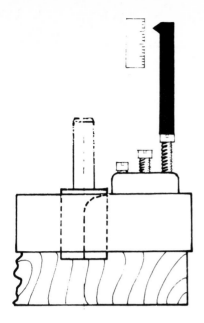

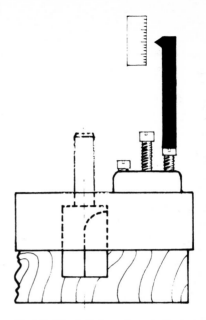

Fig.7.7. (Top left) Stage One, shallow cut. Depth bar locates on long threaded stop.

Fig.7.8. (Top right) Stage Two, second depth position reached. Depth bar locates on medium threaded stop.

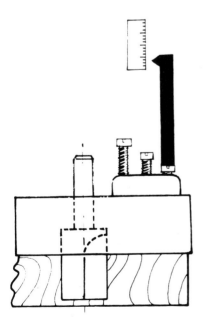

Fig.7.9. (Left) Stage Three, third depth position reached. Depth bar locates on short threaded stop.

The rotary turret stop (Fig. 7.6)

In the previous paragraph we showed the method for setting the
routing depth for a single plunge. However, more often than not the
router is needed to perform at a greater depth than is advisable to work
in one pass of the router. Therefore, we shall now show a typical
multi-stage routing and cutting operation showing the use of the
rotary turret stop. As can be seen from Figs. 7.7-7.9 the turret stops
provide for three alternative depths of working. A ⅓ turn anti-
clockwise of the turret head quickly offers a new depth with the depth
rod engaging on the screw head.

Since changing from one depth to another is only a three-second
operation, fast working is guaranteed and deep working can be
undertaken without overloading the motor. The depth stop screws are
in three lengths and when these are set to their required projection,
back nuts are tightened to prevent them working loose.

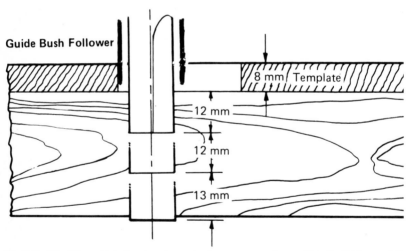

*Fig.7.10. The 36mm thick door is to be cut in three stages as shown. Note the thickness of the
template, which has to be allowed for when setting the depth of plunge.*

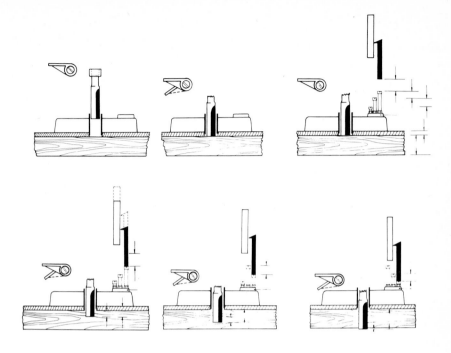

Fig.7.11. (Top left) A suitable cutter is chosen and fitted. In this case, a long-reach cutter, 37mm cut=depth, with diameter of 13mm.

Fig.7.12. (Top centre) Depress plunge lever and carriage so that cutter rests on workpiece, then release lever, to lock in that position.

Fig.7.13. (Top right) The workpiece is to be cut in three stages. 1. Set longest screw on turret depth stop to allow router to penetrate one-third of the workpiece, namely 12mm. 2. Set medium length screw to allow for cutting 12mm deep. 3. Set short screw to allow for cutting 13mm deep.

Fig.7.14. (Bottom left) Switch on motor. To make first cut, depress plunge lever and plunge cut the workpiece down to limit of long set screw. Rout groove guided by the template.

Fig.7.15. (Bottom centre) To make second cut, rotate anti-clockwise turret stop a ⅓ turn. Depress plunging lever and plunge cut to limit on medium screw and repeat routing operation as for the first cut.

Fig.7.16. (Bottom right) To make third cut, rotate turret stop anti-clockwise a ⅓ turn. Depress plunge lever and plunge cut to limit on short screw. The 13mm plunge will pierce the workpiece and allow the routed centre section to drop through. Depress lever, allowing carriage to spring up to original position (as at 7.11). Switch off motor.

Multi-stage cutting

The problem in hand is to rout an aperture in a solid door to provide a cut recess which is to be glazed. Figs. 7.11-7.16 describe graphically and in detail the procedure for routing out a clean-cut aperture to receive glazing beads. The method recommended includes the need for an 8mm thick template stuck, clamped or pinned to the door face (see Fig. 7.10). (Template design and construction is dealt with in Chapter 4.)

Fig.8.1. Removing of unsightly knots and covering of drilled or counterbored holes can be done with the plunge router, if special matching tools are used.

8. Drilling by hand

The very real advantages of being able to drill with a router, have not 'come home' to the average woodworker. In fact the idea of drilling with any tool other than a hand drill or pillar drill could be thought of as a form of heresy! Drilling with a router should, however, only be attempted with a plunging type hand router, which has spring-loaded columns, e.g. the Elu.

The 'plunging' facility in the router creates a number of useful applications which are not available with the conventional router. For example, suitable cutters (from the refs. 2, 3 and 4 shown, page 122 in the Appendix) can produce pre-drilled holes to accept screws and bolts. The holes are clean-cut and parallel and of a far superior quality to the conventionally drilled ones. The secret is the high cutting speed. If the cutter is sharp a fine clean cut, almost polished, is obtained. A word of advice is needed here, however, for it is not advisable to attempt such work in any direction other than downwards. The reason is that it is difficult to obtain a good purchase on the router to plunge the carriage horizontally or in an upwards direction. The plunge drilling router can also provide a useful means of dowel jointing, which is discussed on page 79.

Plunge type cutters

We should mention the importance of cutters used for drilling purposes. These have cutting edges on their bases and, as in the engineering trades, are often termed 'end mill' cutters. With the advent of the plunging router, however, the term 'plunge cut' has been adopted.

The router bit for drilling purposes should ideally have clearance of approximately 20 deg. (ground back from the loading edge). While HSS cutters are usually ground to give a good clearance, small cutters of ¼in. and below are not easy to grind in this way. Solid TC cutters on the other hand present no difficulties in obtaining good relief. These are now often chosen if clean-cut small holes without burn marks are especially required. With this type of cutter it is possible to enter the work from above as well as from the edge. The router motor must necessarily be brought down into the work through the action of a foot pedal in a fixed-head router (such as the Interwood), or by manual pressure in a portable 'plunging' router (such as the Elu).

Drilling blind holes

When drilling blind holes it is usually advisable to limit the first plunge

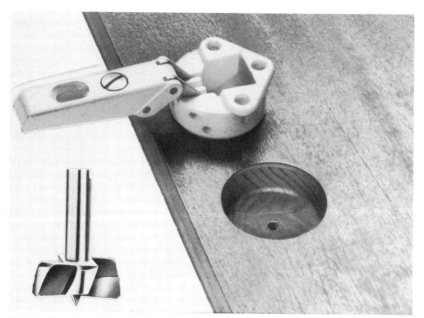

Fig.8.2. By using a Trend Hinge Sinking Cutter Type 421, a most practical method of cutting clean holes to receive circular hinges is obtained.
N.B. *These sinking cutters should only be used with plunging type routers, overhead routers or pillar drills. See also page 127, re cutting speeds.*

to a maximum depth of 1in. Since cutters have little or no helix (spiral fluting) the chips should be cleared by releasing the carriage lock, i.e. lifting the cutter out of the work. If, say, a 1⅝in. hole is required a second plunge will be necessary to take it past the 1in. previously drilled.

The rotary depth stop turret will facilitate this operation, as the router must be held firmly to prevent the second hole 'running off' the position made by the first hole. If two settings on the turret are preset to enable the router to first drill 1 in. and then a further ⅝in., the light ⅓ turn of the turret head can be done with the finger and thumb of the right hand, while the left hand is holding the router firmly to prevent any movement.

Plug and knot-hole borers (see Fig. 8.1)

The removal of an unsightly knots or screw holes in plywood or timber can be carried out most efficiently if a matching pair of plug and hole makers are chosen. These cutters are designed in such a way that a perfect tight fit can be guaranteed. The plug will need a light tape to fit into position. (Drilling, countersinking, counterboring and plugging are dealt with further on page 93.)

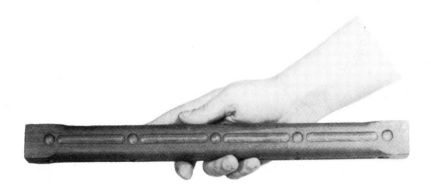

Fig.8.3. Alternative shallow grooves and holes provide attractive possibilities for those engaged in decorative work. Cutter used was a Ref 12/7 radius cutter.

Hinge sinking cutters

Round hinges, particularly in the furniture industry, are very much in common use now, the main advantage being the simplicity with which they can be fixed (see Fig. 8.2). A special range of hinge sinking cutters is available now for use with 'plunging' routers.

Decorative work

The possibilities for decorative applications are unlimited. Cutters

Fig.8.4. The router is inverted to show how an acrylic 'see-through' plate with cross datum lines can be fixed to the router base.

with 'bottom cut' facilities will produce dimples and shaped indentations with attractive results. Combinations of dimples and grooves (as illustrated in Fig. 8.3) on chair legs, lamp standards and so on, present a great challenge to one's creative abilities.

Useful hints for drilling by hand

Feedback of information from the trade, prompts me to mention a few simple but invaluable innovations. First, it is worth mentioning a simple means of ensuring that the router remains still when the carriage is plunged down. If both base and workpiece are slippery a slight movement when plunging will cause an oval hole to be drilled. The solution is to fit a sheet of fine sanding paper to the router base, using double-sided adhesive tape. It's as simple as that!

One minor criticism of drilling with a router is the sighting of the position where the hole is to be drilled. However, the following procedure overcomes this set-back. A 'false' base, made from a clear acrylic sheet, is secured to the router base (with standard fixing screws or double-sided tape). A single plunge drilled hole locates the centre point of the cross, then datum lines are engraved on the outer face and filled with black enamel. The sighting of pre-marked drilling points is now a quick and simple operation (see Fig. 8.4).

Drilling, countersinking, counterboring and plugging (see Figs. 8.5-8.8)

There is now a one-piece tungsten tipped drilling tool available for use with the 'plunging' router which has a triple application. It can be used in either plunging routers or power drills. It is available in three sizes to suit No. 8, 10, and 12 wood screws. Not only will it drill holes, but if brought further down into the workpiece, will countersink them also. Bringing the tool down still deeper gives clean cut apertures or counterbores. The apertures are so accurate and square that cover plugs can be fitted most effectively. (Ref. group 24 range of plug cutters shown in the Appendix, page 128, are suitable for this purpose.)

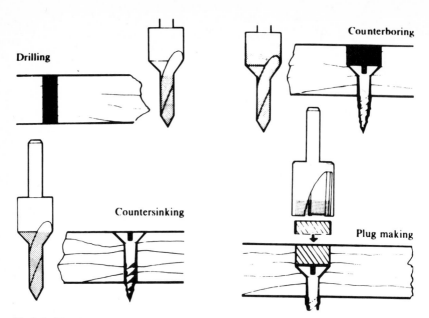

Fig.8.5. (Top left) Drilling tool, ref 62, is drilling a square clean-cut hole.

Fig.8.6. (Below left) The same tool, brought down further into the work, has produced a countersink.

Fig.8.7. (Top right) The same drill taken further still, has produced a counterbored hole.

Fig.8.8. (Below right) A plug-making cutter, ref 24, will produce a plug to cover up a counterbored hole. A light press fit produces a first-class joint.

Fig.8.9. This Elu routing jig incorporates a plunging head, with vertical and lateral movement, and variable stops. It will drill key holes, lock handle shafts and, when swung over, it will rout a shallow recess for the lock plate.

Drilling key holes in wood doors

Devices for drilling holes for ironmongery provide just one more application of the totally underrated router system which is used for making apertures. The clever appliance shown in Fig. 8.9, clamps onto the door edge for drilling key and door handle shafts. When swung over, it will recess a groove to receive the lock plate.

9. Use of arbors

It would be true to say that the router is the most under-rated tool in the woodworking trade. Those who possess them rarely use them to their full potential and so in this chapter we shall look at a whole range of applications and show just how versatile the hand router can be. Some very useful machining applications can be found by fitting the router with arbors instead of cutters. They will accept groovers, slitting blades, trimmers and saw blades and are available in two basic types: the light duty ones (see Figs. 9.1, 9.2 and 9.3) which are designed for such jobs as edge slotting, trimming, recessing for weather strip inserts, and a recent application, slitting double glazed units for reclaiming glass; and heavy duty ones which are used for such work as tongueing and grooving (see Chapter 6), or trimming off flash in the plastics industry. The component parts of the heavy duty arbor, and its various groovers, slotters and blades are shown on page 101. An interesting innovation is the undercut groover for introducing a plastic liner or weatherproof strip (see Figs. 9.4 and 9.5).

These arbors can also be used when the router is mounted beneath the work table (as a mini-spindle, see Chapter 10). In this instance the material is fed into the cutting head and providing safety guards are utilised to conform to health and safety regulations, a full range of new applications is opened up.

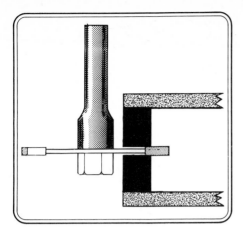

Fig.9.1. Slitting the mastic jointing of a double glazed sealed unit: a narrow necked arbor is used with a TC slitting blade.

Fig.9.2. Slotting a table top for insertion of edge strip: the light duty arbor is fitted with a bush bearing, a TC tipped slotter being mounted by cap screw on its base.

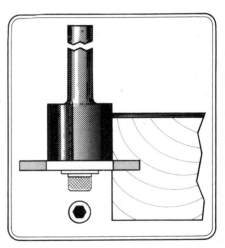

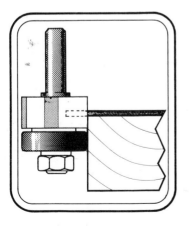

Fig.9.3. Trimming the plastic laminate overlay: a TCT trimmer was used with exact matching bearing beneath.

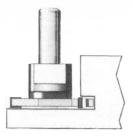

Fig.9.4. (Above) Undercut grooving for weatherstrip insert: groover ref. is 34/10; arbor ref. is 33/10. This arbor threads into the groover (available in various thicknesses).

Fig.9.5. (Right) Undercut groover, when removed from arbor, shows the threaded portion: groover ref. is 34/12.

Reclaiming double glazed units

Owing to the high cost of glass it has now been found to be economical to reclaim damaged units (see Fig. 9.6). The Elu power trimmer has been especially adapted to split the sides of double glazed units in order that the glass can be salvaged and re-used. In fact, most small routers can be used for this purpose, but a false base should be fitted to counterbalance the machine to prevent it tipping and shattering the glass.

Recessing draught excluder strip

There are a number of such products on the general market, but most are unsightly or impermanent. To fit such a weather strip profession-ally is now within the scope of the amateur. An example is given below of a brush strip with a 'keyed' or 'barbed' insertion edge (see Figs. 9.7-9.9). The arbor type 33/9 is fitted with a slotter in the ref. 47/7A-D range, which is bolted to the base of the arbor. A slotter which can cut

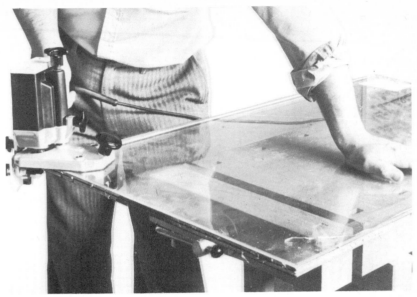

Fig.9.6. Reclaiming glass: an Elu power trimmer type 67 is used to slit double-glazed units. This machine can slit a unit 4 ft square in less than 2 minutes. Thin wedges are fitted behind the tool at approximately 1 ft intervals.

Fig.9.7. (Below) Slotting a table top for insertion of edge strip: the light duty arbor is fitted with a bush bearing, a TC tipped slotter being mounted by cap on its base. Cutter ref. is 47/7B screw.

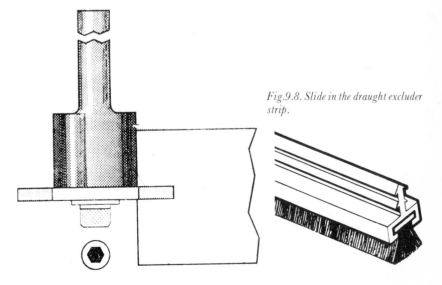

Fig.9.8. Slide in the draught excluder strip.

Fig.9.9. Narrow slot to receive draught excluder.

between 1.5mm and 3mm wide can cope with most recessing work of this nature. If the depth of the router is adjusted up or down, the width of slot can be widened to suit the occasion. (In certain instances the brush strip housing may need to be recessed too.) If the full 9mm slotting depth is acceptable, the round base of the arbor can be used as a guide for running along the board edge. Alternatively, the adjustable side fence can be used.

Heavy duty arbors

Arbors and the tooling used with heavy duty hand routers, namely those above 1½ hp, present a valuable asset on the building site. So often, unforseen machining work becomes necessary, particularly when the joinery shop has a full quota of work. The machine table, which fits into the back of a car boot, can be erected in minutes, and set up to perform such jobs as grooving, rebating, and trimming. The arbor assembly (see Fig. 9.10) with its various groovers and blades (see Fig. 9.11), together with an optional roller bearing for guidance, offers plenty of scope for such operations.

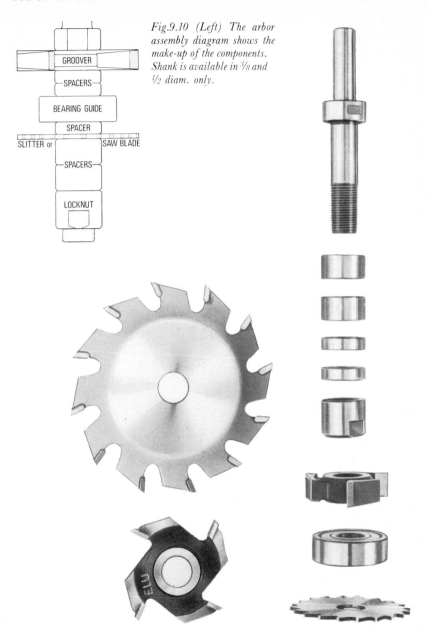

Fig.9.10 (Left) The arbor assembly diagram shows the make-up of the components. Shank is available in ⅜ and ½ diam. only.

GROOVER

SPACERS

BEARING GUIDE

SPACER

SLITTER or   SAW BLADE

SPACERS

LOCKNUT

Fig.9.11. This heavy duty arbor in 'exploded' view is shown with various groovers, slotters, and blades. The bearing shown can be used as a guide running against the board edge.

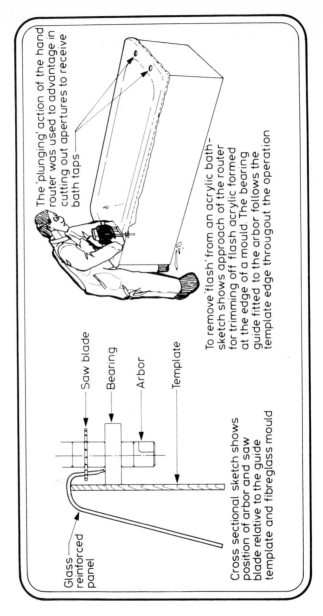

The 'plunging' action of the hand router was used to advantage in cutting out apertures to receive bath taps

To remove 'flash' from an acrylic bath-sketch shows approach of the router for trimming off 'flash' acrylic formed at the edge of a mould. The bearing guide fitted to the arbor follows the template edge througout the operation

Saw blade

Bearing

Arbor

Template

Glass reinforced panel

Cross sectional sketch shows position of arbor and saw blade relative to the guide template and fibreglass mould

Fig.9.12. Trimming off 'flash' from acrylic bath tops.

Trimming off 'flash'

A router is the ideal powered tool for trimming off the edges of 'flash' as it is called in the trade. There are a number of ways in which the router can be applied in conjunction with a template, but Fig. 9.12 shows a system for trimming acrylic bath tops. A template can be fitted over the top of the bath or, as shown in the illustration, on the vertical plane.

A protective sheet of material (not shown) is needed to protect the bath edge from being scratched by the base of the router. There is a definite advantage in a 'plunging' router for this work, because the taps, overflow and waste can all be routed out with the same machine using a cutter of the 421 group, see page 127.

10.   The router as a machine table

Machining work as a whole, is not carried out on the building site, but back in the joinery shop. However, with a light-duty machining table, better described as a light-duty spindle, there are a number of jobs which can be done on the building site. A few of the applications are as follows: production of mouldings for architraves and skirtings, short runs of tongueing and grooving, rebating, tenoning (see Chapter 6 for all), trimming formica edges, edge slotting for draught excluders . . . the list continues indefinitely.

Naturally, we are talking about relatively short runs of work, but how invaluable to be able to carry out such applications on the spot! So often the building specification is subject to modifications and the client requires extras not originally allowed for in the joinery shop.

The equipment one requires consists basically of an inverted hand router (Elu in this instance) fitted into a special table which, while small, is stable and provides a solid working surface. As will be seen from Fig. 10.1, provision is made for an adjustable side fence with spring loaded clamps (Fig. 10.2) to hold the material firm when machining.

These clamps hold the material down while it is being fed in and also constitute protection guards, and as such, are looked on favourably by the Health and Safety authorities. All this equipment can be purchased complete for between £200 and £250, depending on the accessories required. One attraction is that of portability, as it can be taken from site to site in the back of a small van. It is available in 110V and 230V (single phase) to comply with local electricity supply regulations.

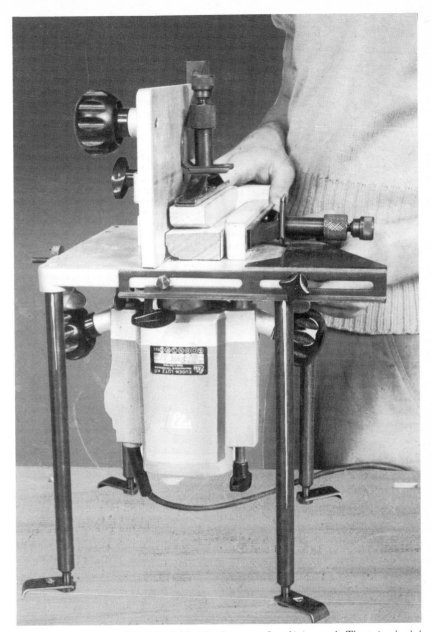

Fig.10.1. This router machine table is ideal for short runs of machining work. The spring-loaded clamps hold the work steady and act as protection guards.

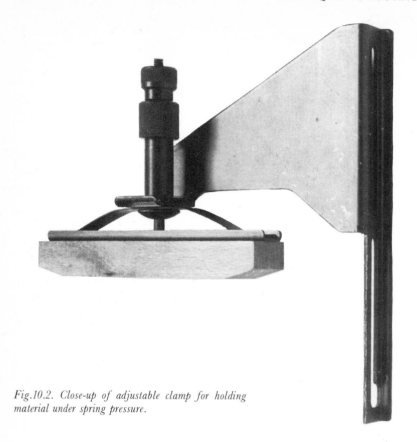

Fig.10.2. Close-up of adjustable clamp for holding material under spring pressure.

Trimming circular components

Fig. 10.3 shows an overlay of plastic being trimmed on a circular component. The cutter (ref. 46/10, page 141 in the Appendix) has the bearing on the underside of the cutter, and this acts as the guide for the material under the laminate.

Direction of feed

Always feed the material in the opposite direction to that in which the cutter is rotating. Remember that when the cutter is projecting

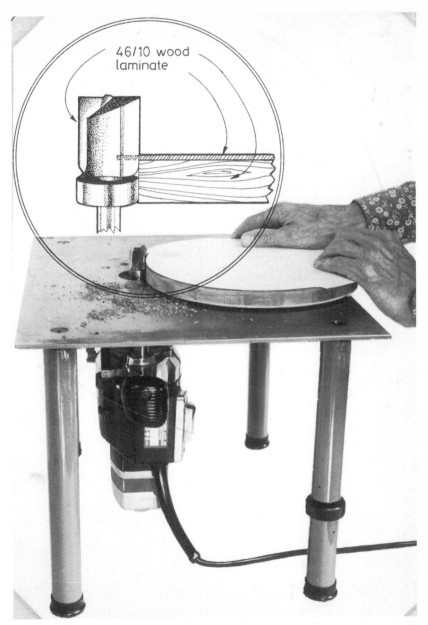

Fig.10.3. The latest 46/10 trimmer. The use of a routing machine table comes 'into its own'. when trimming of laminate edges on a curved workpiece is involved.

Fig.10.4. The small machine table as set up for profiling a child's cot end. A template, secured to the workpiece with double-sided tape, runs against a roller bearing follower mounted over the cutter. Exact alignment is necessary and the table mounting must be carefully secured.

upwards the direction of cut is opposite to that when the cutter is pointing downwards (i.e. when hand routing).

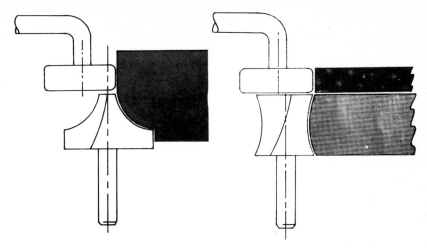

Fig.10.5. and 10.6. The independent overhead bearing system on a small router table, which emphasizes the positions required so that the workpiece can follow the board edge (10.5. left) or template edge (10.6. right). Standard two flute cutters are used as these have bottom-cut clearance. See Appendix.

Machine table with guide roller

For profiling shaped workpieces, such as a plywood cot, see Fig. 10.4, a shaped template is secured to the plywood panels by nails or double sided tape. The template engages on an overhead mounted roller with the cutter fitted to the inserted router immediately below, trimming the plywood to the pattern. If the straight cutter is replaced by a radiused one, a moulded edge can replace the square one (see Fig. 10.5).

Rebating on the machine table

Fig. 10.6 shows once again how the machine table can be firmly fixed in to a carpenter's bench, and in this instance, used to rebate a grandfather clock face over the projecting cutter. The fine adjustment facility on the router is used to obtain the exact depth of cut.

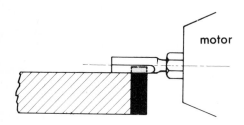

Fig.10.7. A 3/50 10mm
∅ cutter fitted laterally to the
router.

Angular machine table

One accessory for the MOF 96 router is an angular machine table
which clamps to the edge of the workshop table. The cutter protrudes
horizontally (see Fig. 10.7) and the side of the cutter removes the
material.

Fig. 10.8 shows a small window frame being rebated along its outer
edges. Once more, the spring loaded clamp serves dual purpose roles.

Fig.10.8. With the machine table mounted laterally on the workbench, further possibilities are opened up. Here a window is being rebated on all sides.

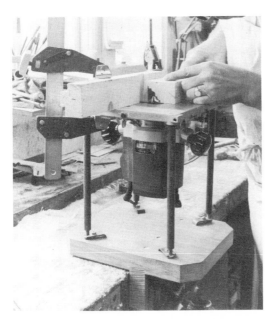

Fig.10.9. The small machine table which is supplied as an accessory with Elu MOF 96 router, is seen fitted to a carpenter's workbench. The strong 'T' shaped base panel enables the machine table to be clamped quickly into the vice of the workbench.

Small mini-spindle

A small machine table, powered by a router, can be most productive. For instance, making one's own mouldings from square battening presents a very real economy in these times of high timber costs. When working narrow material for making, say, window sash bars or picture frame mouldings, a 'suva' clamp (Fig. 10.2) can be fitted to the horizontal fence plate, and a second one will ensure that the material being machined is held firmly against the cutter in both directions (see Fig. 10.1).

An even finish throughout the length of the workpiece can thus be obtained. This can be an important factor when making up frames with

Fig.10.10. The system for trimming hardwood lipping is clearly shown when the pressure clamp is removed to expose the side of the cutter.

mitred corners. The additional safety measures the clamps provide should be mentioned, they both protect the operator from the exposed cutter and conform to safety regulations.

A small router table

The machine table is seen in Fig. 10.9 fitted to a simple wood base, which in turn fits onto a carpenters' bench and is secured firmly in place. A home-made side fence has been fitted, and a compound moulded edge is obtained by passing the material over the projecting cutter. A fine screw feed depth adjuster is rotated in a clockwise or anti-clockwise direction to bring the cutter up or down as required. The cutter used to obtain the mould effect was ref. 7/6 (page 124 in the Appendix), set at varying depths.

Trimming hardwood lipping

The same set-up as for rebating can be used for trimming hardwood lipping. Fig. 10.10 illustrates this clearly. The spring 'suva' clamp has been omitted to give a clearer view of the cutter in relation to the hardwood edging.

Fig.10.11. Cutting out of letters and components can be undertaken on the router table. The use of chamfer cutters with guide pins to finish the edges is now standard practice by sign makers. The illustration shows a 40 deg. chamfer being put on an acrylic letter E.

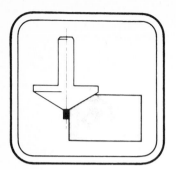

Fig.10.12. A chamfer cutter, type 10F, has a guide pin mounted on its base for following the edge.

Shaping letters (see Fig. 10.11)

Some sign makers prefer to use an inverted router, as opposed to an overhead one. The illustration shows a letter 'E' being bevelled. The cutters used for this purpose have a guide pin fitted to their base (Fig. 10.12). They are ideal for profiling materials which have small intricate shapes, as the guide pin is able to reach right into the corners.

11. Care and maintenance

Previous writings on the 'plunging' router have neglected to emphasise the importance of the cutter, or router bit as it is called. One experienced craftsman in this field says: 'The hand router is only as good as the cutter used in it.' How true this is! A feathery edge on the board is more likely to have been caused by a blunt cutter than a faulty machine.

Selecting cutters

A wide range of cutters in numerous shapes and sizes is on the market and a special wallchart which describes these in an informative manner can be supplied (parts of this chart are reproduced in the Appendix). A brief run down of the various types of cutters follows below.

Straight cutters: these are cutters with single or double flutes, straight edged, and leaving a 90 deg. cut edge.

Shaped cutters: these are used mainly for moulding, bevelling, shaping and panelling.

Grades of cutters: by grades of cutters, we are referring to the metallurgical composition. We will describe for simplicity, the two main types available for hand routing machines.

High speed steel cutters: when they are sharp they will give an exceedingly good finish to the work, but if the material is abrasive in any way, they quickly become blunt and need re-sharpening after a short run of work. The materials which come under the category of non-abrasive are as follows: most natural soft woods, pvc, and acrylic (non-tinted variety). It should be noted that these cutters normally have a back clearance angle of not less than 15 deg. If sharpening is to be carried out, this angle should be maintained to ensure good cutting performance.

Tungsten carbide cutters: these are greatly superior to high speed steel cutters, by virtue of their lasting quality. They are particularly suitable for harder abrasive materials, such as plywood, chipboard, hardboard, fibreglass reinforced plastics, and acrylics (tinted variety). While the complete cutter can be made out of solid tungsten carbide, the normal practice is to braze small sections of tungsten carbide onto all cutting edges (see Fig. 11.1).

The cost of tungsten carbide cutters are, from experience, two to three times that of an HSS cutter, but they last many times as long, depending on the material. Since the time spent in removing the cutter, having it re-sharpened, and refitting it into position, has to be taken into consideration, it is generally more economical from a time saving point of view to use tungsten carbide tipped cutters. They keep their cutting edge much more efficiently and preclude the need for

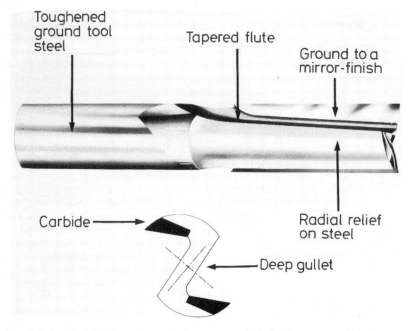

Fig.11.1. A typical TCT two-flute cutter in tungsten carbide. Solid tungsten carbide cutters are also available. While more expensive than the tipped variety, they can be resharpened many times before being discarded. They also have a better 'plunge' facility.

constant resharpening. When tungsten carbide cutters are worn, they should be re-sharpened properly at the correct angle. This too will increase their life span. Cutter maintenance is discussed fully below.

Design factor in a tungsten carbide cutter: the brazing in of the tungsten carbide insert, and the fine grinding of the insert, are important factors in a TC cutter, but the relief and clearance has to be correct if efficient cutting is to be obtained before regrinding becomes necessary.

Solid tungsten cutters: while all the advantages of tungsten tipped cutters apply equally to cutters made completely from tungsten, the solid TC cutters have an additional advantage in that they are less likely to snap under stress because they are ground from a single piece of steel. Their plunge facility is also superior. Cost is, however, somewhat higher than the tipped TC cutters.

Maintenance

Generally speaking it is advisable to send cutters to a reputable cutter sharpening firm, as accurate equipment is needed to refurbish the cutters to a standard as near as possible to their original condition. However, with high speed steel cutters, hand honing with a fine stone can be carried out on the inside flat edge of the cutter, never on the outside radius, as this will alter the clearance angle and ruin the performance. It should be remembered that honing is purely a touching-up operation, and if done regularly after each short to medium run of work, the cutter will give excellent results over a long period. If the cutter is allowed to deteriorate honing will be ineffective, and it will need to be sent to a specialist for regrinding.

The merit in having one's cutters resharpened by a firm with specialised equipment cannot be over-emphasised. So often it is thought that there is a short cut to this problem, and the end results of this attitude are shown clearly in Fig. 11.3. Fig. 11.4 shows how the same cutter appears after it has been reground correctly. Note the excellent relief for clearance of chips.

Re-grinding attachments are available for some hand routers. With these it is possible to sharpen straight cutters effectively, but the setting up of the apparatus is most important, and only a minimal amount of material should be ground off at any one time. Cutting angles must be maintained if success is to be achieved.

Fig.11.2. Cutters being serviced on premises of a saw doctor. They should be reground correctly when their edges have become dull. A cutter needs attention when the cut edge becomes 'feathery' or when the motor is dropping its revs unusually.

Re-sharpening of TCT cutters should not be attempted at all without the correct equipment. Special diamond-impregnated grinding wheels are used by firms with equipment which ensures the correct reliefs are maintained. Each firm charges a different rate for the job, but providing the tungsten tip is still intact, the cost for sharpening is approximately £2.00 a time (mid-1980).

It is not generally realised that the shanks of router cutters should be maintained smooth, and as near to the condition as received from the factory. A cutter shank with a burr on it will result in an inaccurate cut

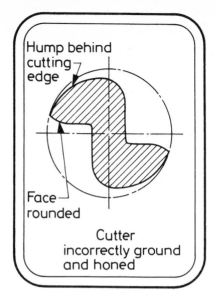

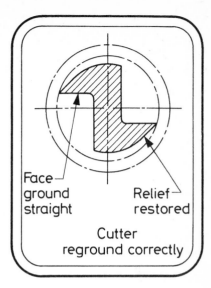

Hump behind
cutting
edge

Face
rounded

Cutter
incorrectly ground
and honed

Face
ground
straight

Relief
restored

Cutter
reground correctly

Fig.11.3. Cutter incorrectly ground and honed.

Fig.11.4. Cutter reground correctly.

and may also cause vibration. With the larger cutters bearings on the motor may be adversely affected owing to the inbalance. Over-tightening of the collet often distorts it, and causes grooves in the cutter shank. Dirt or grit adhering to the shank will have a similar effect. It is therefore important that the cutter shank is regularly examined.

Feed speed relative to work

It is important to look after your routing machine by not overloading it. A clear sign that the machine is being overloaded is a drastic drop in the revolutions of the spindle. Feed rate therefore can be judged by the sound of the motor. In time the operator will acquire a 'feel' for the router, and a feed speed relative to the work will come to him naturally. It will be found that a narrow cutter can be used at a higher speed than a wider one.

A guide line for assessing cutting depth is that the depth of cut should not exceed the diameter of the cutter. If this principle is not adhered to when routing hard material the cutter may snap. If the cutter is inclined to burn the material it is a sign that either the cutter is blunt or that the feed speed is too slow.

It is impossible to give a hard and fast rule about recommended cutting speeds because conditions vary from job to job. Generally speaking, however, a **a**in. diameter cutter requires a free running speed of between 20,000 and 24,000 rpm for the best results. Conversely, a cutter of ¾in. diameter needs a speed of between 14,000 and 20,000 rpm. An important point to remember is that if the router is underpowered the cutting speed under load will be drastically reduced and a poor performance is the obvious result. A correct periphery speed using a sharp cutter will ensure a good finish. A feathery finish on the groove edges is the usual sign that attention is needed in this area. Several passes with the router should be made if a single deep pass causes the revs. to drop below 70 per cent of the free running speed.

Routers should always be fed in the opposite direction to that in which the cutter is rotating. Fig. 11.5 shows the direction of feed when the router is overhead, i.e. in portable routing/profiling. When using a fixed head router (spindle) with the cutter pointing upwards through the table, the material is fed in the opposite direction.

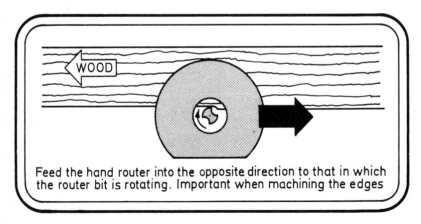

Fig.11.5. Important: whether for portable working or when using the router on the machine stand, the direction of feed must oppose the cutter direction when profiling.

To summarise then, there are five important points to consider when setting the feed speed to achieve the best results:

Don't feed the router too slowly as it will burn the material rather than cut it;

Don't overtighten the collet chuck;

Don't feed the router too fast. The finish will be inferior.

Don't overload the motor, but keep up the motor revolutions.

Don't try to service the router yourself; send it to an accredited service agent.

Do use protective goggles when working, especially with particle board. The dust can damage your eyes.

Do switch off and unplug the router while changing the cutter or accessories: an elementary precaution, but so often ignored

Appendix

One flute cutters – 2/1 to 2/6

These cutters are ideal for engraving and shallow work. Because of the narrow stem, extra care is needed when using the TCT version.

Two flute cutters – 3/1 to 4/10

Two flute cutters give a cleaner finish than their one flute counterparts, and at the right feed speed will give a clean cut edge to the work. Use a TCT version if the material is abrasive. Solid tungsten cutters (with a prefix S) will give a better plunging cut and are less likely to snap under stress.

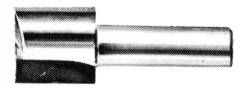

'V' groove and engraving cutters – 11/1 to 11/5, 12/3, S47/70 and 11/50

This range of cutters offers the most possibilities for free hand engraving and fine decorative work. They are used most extensively for mould and panelling work.

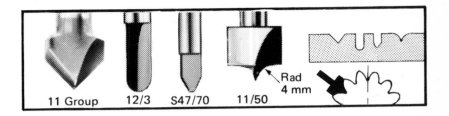

Radius cutters – 12/3 to 12/7, 13/1 to 13/3, and 15/1

These cutters in their narrowest diameters can be used for engraving. In larger sizes, they are used for producing moulded edges, drip grooves under window-sills; largest sizes for door handles and radiused cut-outs, such as ash trays and bowls. They can be used on the hinged section of a drop leaf table, (see Chapter 2).

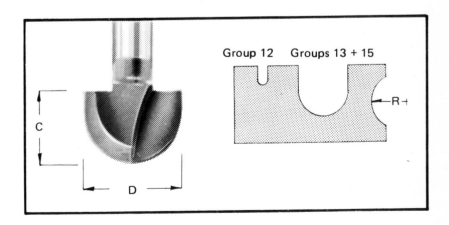

Ovolo cutters – 7/2 to 7/6

This is the most popular cutter for edge moulding work. It is also used for panelling. Attractive shapes can be produced for picture frames, architraves, skirtings and decorative panels. The 7/5 cutter offers a shape which pairs up with cutter ref. 6/5 for window bars.

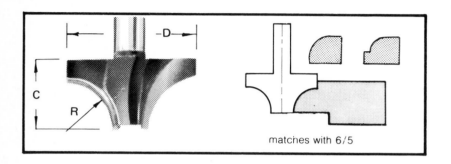

Rounding over cutters – 7E/1 to 7E/5

Similar to the ovolo cutter but with a plain radiused edge without a step. These are popular moulding cutters for free hand working.

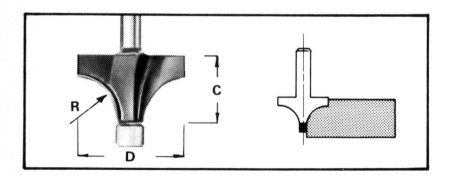

Ovolo (beading) cutters – 7D/1 to 7D/3

Very popular for free hand moulding work. Attractive edging moulds can be applied to board edges giving a pleasing effect. (Opposite)

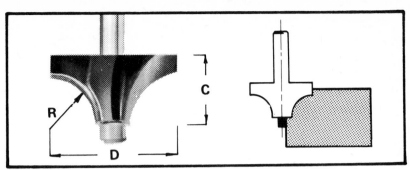

Rebate cutters – 8D/1 and 8D/2

A useful cutter for forming rebates on board edges as the pilot guide follower will easily follow small radii on shaped workpieces. This cutter is also a time saver when the odd rebate has to be machined. It avoids setting up of fences etc. for one-off jobs.

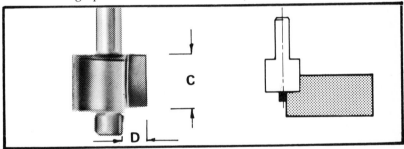

Roman ogee – 8E/1 and 8E/2

This cutter gives a decorative moulded edge and is becoming increasingly popular for carrying out reproduction work. Like the other cutters with guide pins, the edge of the material is followed without the need for a side fence on the router.

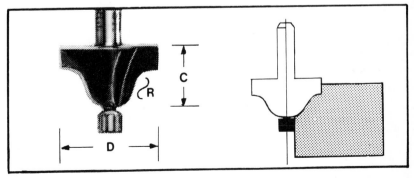

Chamfer cutters – 10H/1 and 10H/2
Frequently used for decorative and practical purposes on outside woodwork, sills and frames. The sign making trades use them extensively for putting a chamfer on letters made from acrylic.

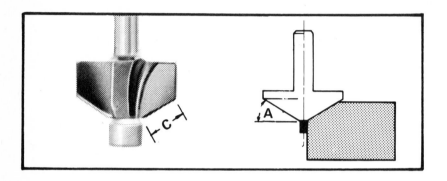

Cove cutters – 13F/1 to 13F/3
These profiling cutters are ideal for edging panels, boards and picture frames, to give a decorative effect. One useful application is for putting a mould on the hinged section of a drop-leaf table (as an alternative to cutter type 12).

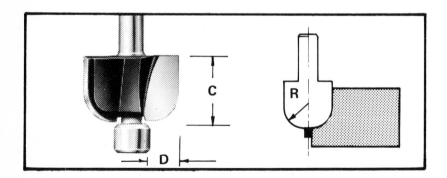

Dovetail cutters – 31/1 to 31/7, also 32/1 to 32/3
Mainly used for producing dovetails on housings and corner joints, when a strong fit is required; also popular for male dovetail tenons at the end of shelves and uprights. The ref. 32 group cutter is designed for staircase housings. (Opposite)

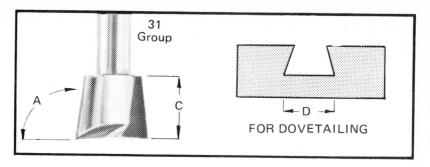

31
Group

A

C

D

FOR DOVETAILING

Hinge sinking cutter – 421/20 to 421/35

This cutter is designed for sinking circular hinges (such as Blum and Heinze types). It is designed for drilling laminate and melamine finished worktops. It can be used at speeds up to 18,000 rpm, but gives its best at 5,000-12,000 rpm.

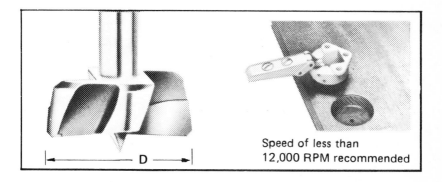

D

Speed of less than
12,000 RPM recommended

Plunge drill countersink (TC tipped) – Sizes No 8 (Ref 62/80), No 10 (Ref. 62/10) and No 12 (Ref. 62/12)

This unique tool can be used in drilling machines or hand plunging routers for drilling holes up to 20mm deep, and countersinking them. If the tool is lowered further, it provides a counterbored hole. Drill and countersink parts are tungsten carbide tipped, thus making them ideal for drilling and countersinking abrasive materials such as chipboard and plywood etc. (Overleaf)

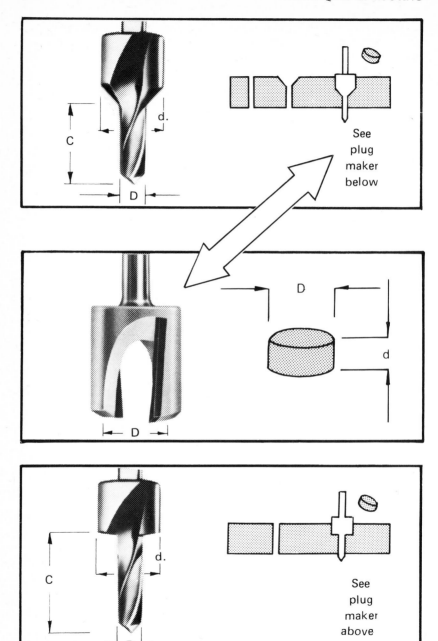

Plug maker (TC tipped) – 24/80, 24/10 and 24/12

Using the combination tools shown in group refs. 62 or 63, screw holes can be drilled and counterbored in one operation. They are then ready to receive the exact matching plug made by a type 24 plug making cutter. These can also be used to fill holes to cover unsightly knots in skirtings and architraves. Plugs are designed to 'light press' in with thumb. Being tungsten carbide tipped, they are suitable for making plugs from abrasive materials, such as melamine covered board, hardwood, etc. (Opposite centre)

Plunge drill counterbore (TC tipped) – 63/80, 63/10 and 63/12

This counterbore with tungsten carbide tips on both drill part and counterbore portion is manufactured in one piece. It is ideal for shopfitters and furniture manufacturers. The counterbored hole can be plugged with a push-fit pellet, provided by plug making cutters, refs. 24/80 – 24/12. (Opposite below)

Panelling cutter – 18/1

This cutter is designed for flat panelling work and gives an attractive finish on hardwood doors, cabinets, etc.

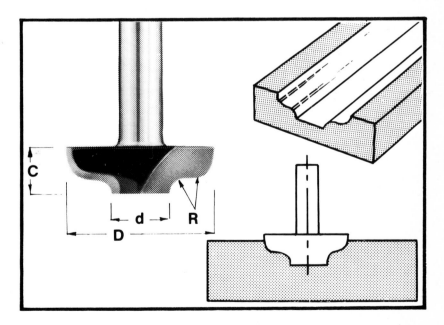

Ogee mould cutter – 19/1, 19/2 and 19/20

The 19/20 can be used for decorative work. It has recently been introduced from the USA for use in a router lathe, to produce decorative legs for chairs, tables, etc.

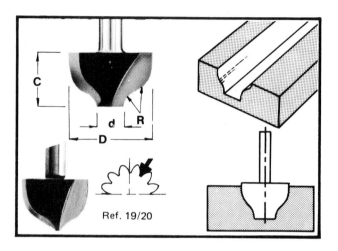

Ref. 19/20

Flat roman ogee – 22/1

As with the classic mould cutter, the flat roman ogee now fills a need in the trade. It is useful for profiling, e.g. 'cappings' on decorative handrails.

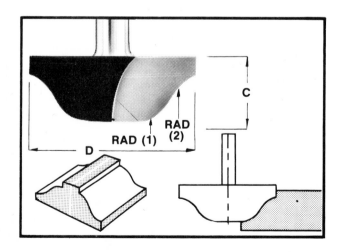

Classic panel and mould cutter – 20/2 and 20/3

This cutter gives a really decorative finish, and fills a need for reproduction and restoration work.

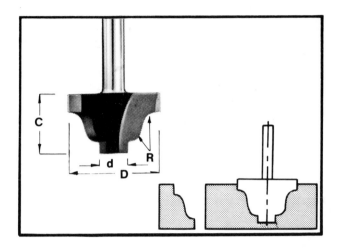

Rabbetting cutter – 46/30

With this guided rabbetting cutter, a 9.5mm ($\frac{3}{8}$in.) rebate is obtained. If a 16mm ($\frac{5}{8}$in.) Ø bearing is introduced, an 8mm (5/16 in.) rebate is obtained.

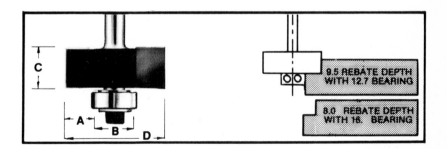

Roman ogee – 46/23 and 46/24

Apart from the roman ogee mould obtained with a 12.7mm ($\frac{1}{2}$in.) Ø bearing fitted as standard, other shallower mould effects are obtained when a 16mm ($\frac{5}{8}$in.) or 20mm Ø bearing is used. (Overleaf)

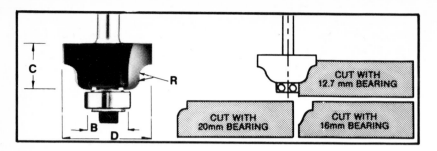

Combination, rounding over ovolo cutter – 46/13 to 46/15

With this range of cutters, two sets of guide bearings are supplied as standard, enabling two applications to be carried out. With 12.7m ($\frac{1}{2}$in.) Ø bearing, an ovolo mould is obtained; with a 16mm ($\frac{5}{8}$in.) Ø bearing, a 'rounded over' shape is produced.

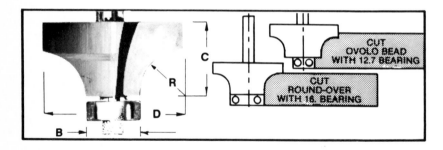

Rounding over/chamfer cutter – 46/40

This cutter was produced with skirtings and architraves in mind. It fills a need for 'on-sight' work, when builders need to run off 'job lots' of skirtings and architraves. The choice of two bearings gives added scope.

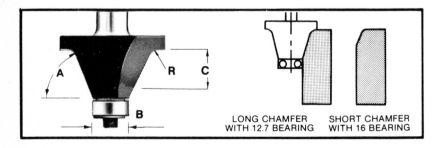

Cove moulding cutter – 46/26 to 46/28

Apart from the cove mould obtained with the standard 12.7mm ($\frac{1}{2}$in.) Ø bearing fitted, shallow radiused coves are obtained when a 16mm ($\frac{5}{8}$in.) Ø or 20mm Ø bearing is fitted.

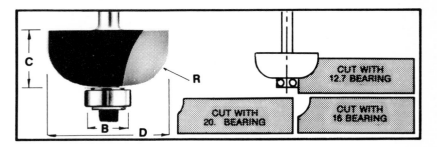

Raised panelling cutter – 46/35

When panelling or reproduction work requires a flat chamfer effect this moulding cutter can prove invaluable.

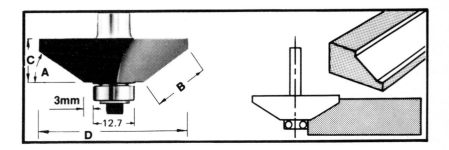

Undercut groovers – 34/10 to 34/12

These groovers, which are threaded into arbors (33/10), enable an undercut to be made in inaccessible corners. Mainly used in sinking weatherstrip, they have other applications, such as recessing iron-mongery and electric cable. (Overleaf)

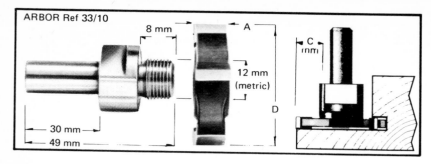

Light duty edge slotters – 33/9 and 47/7A to 47/7D

These slotting blades are supplied for fitting to an arbor for light grooving in the edges of table tops, worktops, etc., where a T section knock-in barbed edge strip is to be fitted. Supplied in four slot widths to accommodate varying sizes of webbed edge strip. The arbor is circular and can be used as a guide.

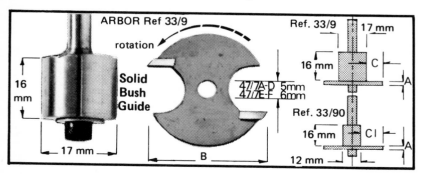

Light duty trimmers – 33/6, 34/6 and B33/6B

These trimmers are available with separate arbor and bearing. They are a substitute for the one-piece trimming cutters with bearings fitted as an integral unit.

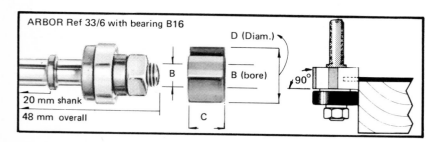

Tongue and groove sets – 334 and 335

This set, complete with arbor, enables the tongue and groove operation to be carried out with heavy duty routers, overhead routers and small spindles. The groovers are suitable for running at speeds of between 7,000 and 20,000 rpm. The set incorporates two four-winged TCT groovers and an arbor with adjustable spacers. See Fig.6.6.

Heavy duty slitter and groover – 34/1 to 34/3

While these can be used with heavy duty hand routers, they are becoming increasingly popular for light spindle work, e.g. when the router is mounted in a work bench (inverted position). Rebating, slotting, slitting and cutting can be carried out, with numerous industrial applications.

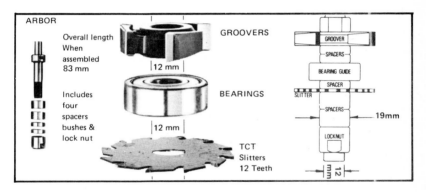

Spiral plunge profile cutter – 50/05 to 50/08

This cutter is used extensively for cutting holes and slots in aluminium extrusions. On other materials such as acrylic and PVC it is an ideal tool for light profiling and cutting.

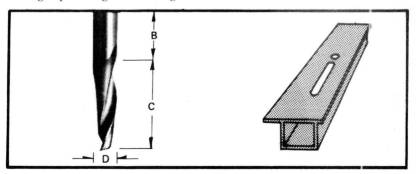

Fibre-glass cutter – S 49/1

Although very popular for cutting re-inforced fibre-glass plastics, it can also be applied to metal and wood. When used portably in a power tool, it becomes a rasp or deburring tool.

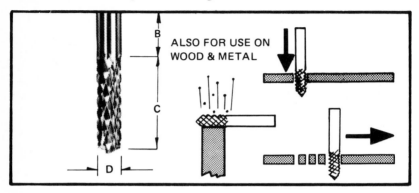

Staff bead cutters and jointers – 9/1 to 9/4 also 8/10 and 8/11

The 9 group forms a half round bead and is mainly for decorative purposes on cabinet doors but is also most useful for rounding over the edges of shelves, picture frames and table tops, etc. The 8 group offers an invaluable jointing system to provide reliable tongued joints.

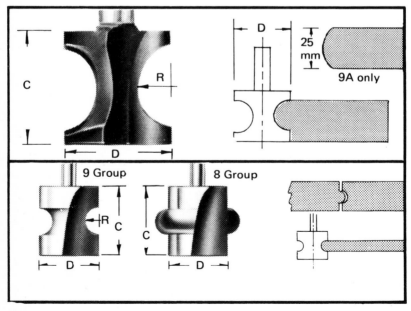

Chamfer cutters – 10/1 to 10/2

These cutters can be used for chamfering boards up to 1in. thick. Having a bottom cut, they are used additionally for centre panelling and decorative work.

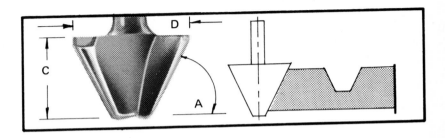

Scribing cutter – 6/5

This cutter is basically designed for the window industry, and offers a much needed jointing system for window mullions and transoms. It pairs with the ovolo cutter, ref. 7/5.

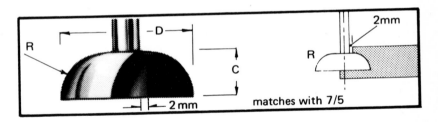

Edge trimmers – 46/2, 46/20 and 46/22

These are carefully constructed with helical cutting edges with the guide bearing being similar in diameter to that of the cutter. Intended mainly for trimming laminated plastic, veneers, etc., after bonding, they enable trimming to be carried out without using a guide fence.

They are especially useful when small dimension, varying contours are to be followed, but bear in mind that the finished trimming cut is only as good as the edge which the bearing has followed. (Overleaf)

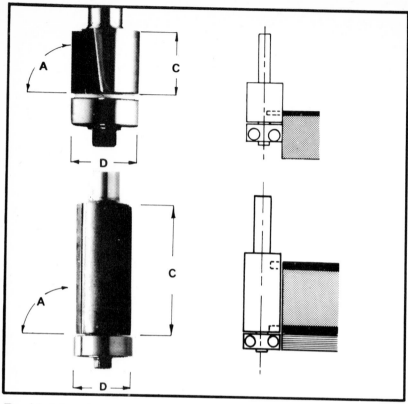

Double trimming cutters – 46/7

A time-saving cutter for trimming the over-lapping edges on the top and bottom surfaces of laminated boards in one operation. The sleeved bearing follows the board between the two laminates producing a perfect finish on the plastic surfaces.

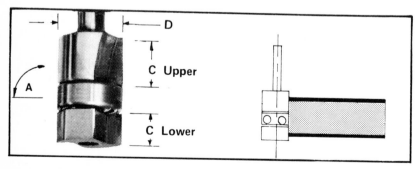

Bevel trimmers – 47/3 and 47/6A to 47/6C

These are supplied as an alternative to the straight 90° cutters for trimming laminates, etc., where an angle is preferred on the finished edge. Supplied in 80°, 60°, 45° and 30°. A side fence follower is required to guide the cutter parallel to the edge.

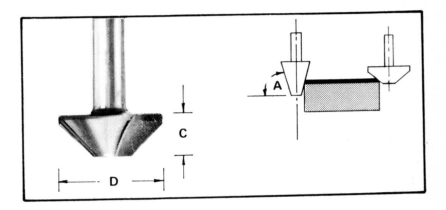

Combination trimmers – 47/5 and 47/7

A very economical cutter, as it will perform three functions for those trimming laminates. It will trim the overlay at 90° and 60°. Furthermore, the base of the cutter can be used for trimming the vertical edge of the lipping.

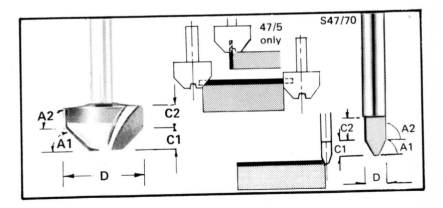

Pierce and trim cutters – 47/4, 47/8, 47/45 and S48/40

These cutters are designed to cut out 'pockets' below the laminate working top, e.g. when tap holes need to be inserted. They will pierce and drill the material and cut out the aperture using the base of the cutter as a guide follower. The S48/40 is made of solid carbide and is designed to edge trim only.

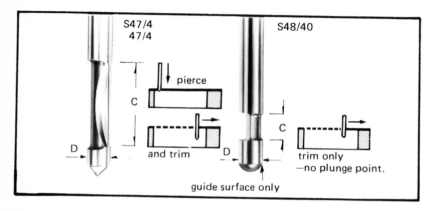

Bevel trimming cutter – 46/3 and 46/6A-C

Similar to the type 46/2, these trimmers have roller bearings to follow the board edge. They offer a choice of showing a wider edge line, when the laminate is trimmed at angles between 30° and 80°.

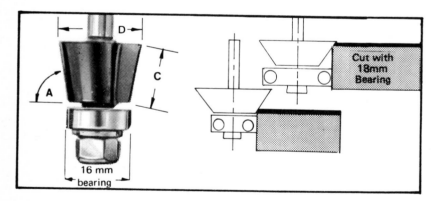

Template profile cutter – 46/9 to 46/11

This rather unusual cutter has a roller bearing mounted at the top.

In this instance, the ball bearing follower has been fitted above the cutter so that a template or pattern can be fitted on top of the workpiece and an exact replica produced. Ideal for one-off jobs where the original sample can be used as the pattern avoiding the necessity of making a template.

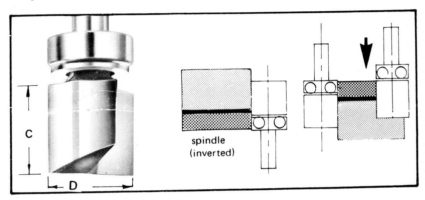

90° Trimming and slotting cutter – 47/1

These cutters are specially designed for the 90 deg. trimming of laminated plastics, veneers, hardboard facings, etc., after they have been bonded to the main board or table top, work top, etc.

The bolt fitted to the base of the cutter is to accommodate a slotting blade. In one operation the laminate is trimmed flush with the edge of the workpiece and a slot accurately machined to accept a T barbed edge strip which can be knocked into the slot. A side fence (or guide if a shaped board is used) will be needed as a guide to engage the trimmer flush with the board edge.

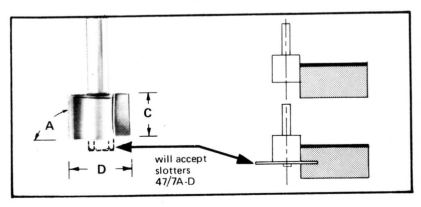

90° Trimmer – 47/2

This cutter has the advantage of being able to trim both vertical lipping (using the bottom cutting edge) and also the overlapping horizontal edge of the laminate or other bonded material (using the vertical cutting edge). Normal practice is to trim the vertical lip, bond the top surface, then trim the lipping. From experience, this cutter has also been found ideal for rebating board, acrylics and aluminium.

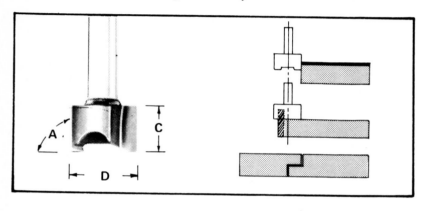

For further information about the cutters shown in the Appendix, contact: Trend Machinery & Cutting Tools Ltd, Unit N, Penfold Works, Imperial Way, Watford, Herts. WD2 4YY

INDEX